"Then Gibbs Said to Riggins..."

The Best Washington Redskins Stories Ever Told

Jim Gehman

TRIUMPH
BOOKS

Library of Congress Cataloging-in-Publication Data

Gehman, Jim, 1960–
    Then Gibbs said to Riggins—: the best Washington Redskins stories ever told / Jim Gehman.
        p. cm.
    ISBN 978-1-60078-270-1
    1. Washington Redskins (Football team)—Anecdotes. 2. Washington Redskins (Football team)—History. I. Title. II. Title: Best Washington Redskins stories ever told.
    GV956.W3G45 2009
    796.332'6409753—dc22

                                                                    2009010032

This book is available in quantity at special discounts for your group or organization. For further information, contact:

Triumph Books
542 South Dearborn Street
Suite 750
Chicago, Illinois 60605
(312) 939–3330
Fax (312) 663–3557
www.triumphbooks.com

Printed in U.S.A.
ISBN: 978-1-60078-270-1
Design by Patricia Frey
Editorial production and layout by Prologue Publishing Services, LLC
Photos courtesy of AP Images unless otherwise indicated

For my dad, Ardell Gehman. Thanks for everything.

And for the men who have coached and played for the Washington Redskins. And for the loyal fans who have supported the Redskins throughout the years.

table of
contents

foreword

As a kid growing up in Texas during the 1960s, I loved the Houston Oilers and hated the Dallas Cowboys so much that I rooted for the Washington Redskins in their big rivalry games every year. Which, to be honest, was not very popular with all of my buddies. It could be because of all that cheering for the Redskins that, when I came to Washington in 1974, I really felt right at home. George Allen made me feel that way. I was very honored to be a part of such a glorious history. The great players who had come before me, those I played with, and those who have come since, I feel all of us have one thing in common: the love of the game. It's bigger than we are! This book goes behind the articles to the actual players and tells their stories as they saw it during the game.

Jim Gehman, who has spent many years covering the National Football League, has captured these individual stories that most people have never heard before. His depth of understanding for the players can only come from someone who has true love for the game. He breaks down many of the great years, great players, and great coaches. Frankly, he hasn't missed too much. I think you will enjoy this book from cover to cover. Especially if you are one among the best fans in the world: Redskins fans. Because once you read this, you will learn so much more about the many wonderful, talented gentlemen who have played and coached for this incredible franchise. You will also gain an appreciation for Redskins football history and those people who have played a part in it.

I hope you enjoy the book as much as I did, because I learned things that I didn't even know. One thing that I do know, however, is that I will always be a Redskin.

Go Skins!

—Mark Moseley

acknowledgments

I would like to thank Andre Collins, David Elfin, Lindsay Entsminger, Doris Gehman, Joe Horrigan, Alex Lubertozzi, Mark Moseley, Jerry Olsen, Rick Snider, and whoever invented the computer's spell check for their assistance and contributions.

I also wish to thank Tom Bast, Michael Emmerich, Adam Motin, Josh Williams, and the staff at Triumph Books for the leadership they have shown throughout this project.

introduction

Beginning in 1932, they called Boston, Massachusetts, home for five seasons—the first year as the Braves and the final four as the Redskins. But on February 13, 1937, just two months after losing to Green Bay 21–6 in the 1936 NFL Championship Game, team owner George Preston Marshall moved the franchise to the nation's capital, and the Washington Redskins were born.

In their first game in their new home on September 16 at Griffith Stadium, 19,941 fans—over 10,000 more than they drew during their final two home games in Boston combined—witnessed the Redskins beat the New York Giants, 13–3.

Behind the league's leading rusher, Cliff Battles, and its leading passer, Sammy Baugh (a rookie from Texas Christian University), head coach Ray Flaherty's club would follow up with seven more victories to finish the regular season with an 8–3 record. They met the Bears in Chicago on December 12 to play for the 1937 NFL title.

"Slingin' Sammy" performed like anything but a rookie in the championship game. He passed for a record 354 yards and three touchdowns to lead the Redskins past the Bears 28–21 for Washington's first championship.

The Redskins played in the title game two more times during the Flaherty era. In 1940 they were beaten, crushed, and embarrassed by the Bears, 73–0. They got revenge two seasons later, however. After posting a near-perfect 10–1 record and outscoring their opponents 227–102, the Redskins topped Chicago, 14–6, in the 1942 NFL Championship Game.

They returned to the 1943 title game but fell short again against the Bears, 41–21. And the Redskins came as close as they could get against the Cleveland Rams in the 1945 championship game (15–14). But from that moment on, Washington could have been mistaken for Mudville with the "Mighty Casey" standing in the batter's box and continually striking out for the next 25 years!

The Redskins had just four winning seasons during that bleak quarter-century. Eleven head coaches, including Pro Football Hall of

Famers Curly Lambeau (1952–1953) and Vince Lombardi (1969) could not get them into the playoffs.

Washington's absence in the postseason came to an end, however, when another head coach who would be enshrined into the Hall of Fame, George Allen, arrived in 1971. A 24–20 playoff loss to San Francisco concluded his first campaign. The following year ended with an NFC championship trophy on owner Jack Kent Cooke's mantle and a 14–7 loss to Miami in Super Bowl VII.

Another coach whose bust can be found in the Canton, Ohio, shrine led the Redskins to their next four Super Bowl appearances. Beginning in 1982, Joe Gibbs' second season in Washington, the Redskins topped Miami, 27–17, in Super Bowl XVII. A year later in Super Bowl XVIII, the then–Los Angeles Raiders squelched any chance on back-to-back titles by ripping the Redskins 38–9. Washington claimed two more Lombardi Trophies during the coach's first tenure: in 1987 they dumped Denver, 42–10, in Super Bowl XXII, and in 1991 they beat Buffalo, 37–24, in Super Bowl XXVI.

Two NFL championships and three Super Bowl titles sandwiching a playoff-deprived 25-year period help make the Redskins one of the most unique teams in the history of professional football. Washington also enjoys arguably the most loyal fan base in the NFL and, as you will read, has a collection of former players who appreciated both aspects while wearing the Burgundy and Gold.

chapter 1

Joe Gibbs: Three Super Bowl Titles, One Hall of Fame Bust

They Hired Joe *Who*?

There is no question that Joe Gibbs paid his dues!

After beginning his career in 1964 as a graduate assistant at his alma mater, San Diego State, Gibbs would go on to coach the offensive line and running backs, and be an offensive coordinator at Florida State, USC, and Arkansas before joining Don Coryell's staff with the NFL's St. Louis Cardinals in 1973. After five seasons under the arch, it was on to the Tampa Bay Buccaneers and then to the San Diego Chargers.

Seventeen years!

But when Jack Kent Cooke named him the head coach of the Redskins on January 13, 1981, Washington's fans and even some of its players asked, "Who is he?"

Gibbs tried to answer that question a few weeks after replacing Jack Pardee during an interview with the *Washington Post*. "Everyone is trying to put together what I'm like. They want to get a feel for the type of person I am," said Gibbs. "But I'm just trying to be myself. I think that comes over pretty quickly. Ultimately, the most important effect I'll have on this world is not how many games I win, but the kind of relationships I have with people. People interest me. I would have to be in some kind of people business if I wasn't coaching. But I'm convinced I am here in this world to do the job I'm doing."

Head coach Joe Gibbs returned to the Redskins in 2004 after winning three Super Bowl championships during his first stint in Washington.

Some of the Redskins players, a veteran-laden team since George Allen began patrolling Washington's sideline in 1971, wondered if they would have a job. Or would the new coach clean house after the team had gone 6–10 the previous season and missed the playoffs for the fourth consecutive year?

"I know people are waiting to see what I do and how I conduct myself. Anyone who forms an opinion about me before I can start doing my job is doing everyone a disservice," Gibbs said. "People have a misconception about this whole situation. I'm not going into this feeling I have to cut older players. That's not how it's going to work. I've been warned that the heart of this team, the veterans, were worried that I was coming in here to get rid of them. But I'm selfish. I don't care if a guy is 20 or 50, if he can play, I'm keeping him. I just want players who want the team to win as badly as I do.

"Age will never be the single determining factor in cutting a player. It will be weighed, of course, along with a lot of other things. I want what is best for the team now and in the future."

Gibbs was confident about the team's future and shelved any speculation that there would be problems between him and general manager Bobby Beathard, who had reportedly clashed with Pardee.

"I am in charge of two things a coach has to be in charge of," said Gibbs. "I hire the staff and I determine the roster. If you don't have those powers, it won't work, and I have them here. The draft is another sticky situation at a lot of places because the coach says he has to have say over the players who could get him fired. Here, Bobby heads the draft, but we are going to have input. The assistant coaches are going to work out the possible prospects, and it will be talked over by everyone, so when we take a guy, we can all live with it.

"I've been involved in three different pro situations. At Tampa Bay, John McKay determined everything. At St. Louis, management had the power. At San Diego, it was shared between the coach and the general manager. Here, it's slightly different because of Bobby's input into the draft. But it's enough like the Chargers to convince me it will be a success. The Chargers are winners, and we will be, too."

"I'm a Washington Redskin"

Given his reputation for having a steadfast work ethic, Joe Gibbs could have worked laying tracks for the first transcontinental railroad in an earlier life.

That, along with the unquestioned leadership he displayed as the head coach of the Redskins for 12 seasons, from 1981 to 1992, and the success that the team earned and enjoyed during that period—eight playoff appearances and three Super Bowl championships—who else would team owner Daniel Snyder have asked to perform the Heimlich on his suffocating franchise in 2004?

But why would Gibbs want to return to Washington? Why even remotely risk tarnishing his Hall of Fame career?

"My decision to return to coaching after 12 years away was the result of a long process of reflection, prayer, and discussion with my family. This was a huge step, and I was well aware of the challenge. It was daunting, to say the least," Gibbs wrote in *Hail Redskins*. "But when I returned to Redskin Park on January 8, 2004, any doubts I might have had about the wisdom of my decision were put to rest. That was the day I was introduced—for the second time—as head coach of the Washington Redskins."

During the 11 seasons that followed Gibbs' retirement, five men patrolled the sideline for the Redskins: Richie Petitbon, Norv Turner, Terry Robiske [three games in 2000], Marty Schottenheimer, and Steve Spurrier. Collectively, they had three winning campaigns and appeared in the postseason only once.

"While I fully understood the magnitude of the task at hand and the fact that there was no guarantee of success, I knew I had done the right thing [by returning to Washington]," Gibbs wrote. "There are a lot of football teams and coaching jobs, but there is no team and no job quite like this one. The Washington Redskins are one of the greatest franchises in all of professional sports. The team has a rich tradition that I came to appreciate and embrace. I felt fortunate to coach the Redskins from 1981 through 1992. Given the opportunity to return by owner Daniel Snyder, I feel fortunate again. I just hope we can achieve the same level of success.

"Even in my years away from football, when I was operating my racing team in Charlotte, North Carolina, and winning NASCAR championships, I still had an emotional bond with the Redskins and the Washington fans. When you share the experience of winning three Super Bowls and you see that pride reflected in the community, that feeling never leaves you. Over the past decade, I was approached by a number of NFL teams, asking if I would consider a return to coaching. Each time I said no. In my heart, I think the only job I could have taken is this one. I'm a Washington Redskin."

The Coach Says His Good-Byes

The first time that Joe Gibbs retired as Washington's head coach occurred on March 5, 1993. He had led the Redskins for 12 seasons, compiling a 124–60 regular-season record, a 16–5 mark in the playoffs, and captured three Super Bowl titles.

However, that success came at a cost.

"I left the Redskins after the 1992 season because I was whipped, physically and emotionally. The stories about our coaching staff working until 4:00 in the morning, living on candy bars and pizza, were no exaggeration," Gibbs explained in *Hail Redskins*. "It drained me to the point where, finally, it was necessary for me to walk away."

Gibbs walked away with enough memories to fill the Smithsonian Institution.

"There are moments you experience as a coach," Gibbs said, "that you cannot experience anywhere else. By 'moments,' most people would assume I'm referring to our three Super Bowl wins—the moment when the game ended and the celebration began. I remember those moments, but it is the relationships I cherish most of all.

"I remember going back on the field after one of our Super Bowls. The stadium was empty, the field was deserted, and Charles Mann, our great defensive end, was there looking around. He said, 'You know, Coach, getting here was the fun.' It was so true. Getting there, building the team, climbing that mountain, was something we all shared. That was the fun, meeting that challenge."

Gibbs' second tenure as Washington's head coach could have been considered challenging and, to a degree, successful. After four seasons, 2004 to 2007, he announced his second retirement on January 8, 2008, just three days after being beaten by Seattle in the NFC wild-card playoff game, 35–14. And even though he led the Redskins to the playoffs twice during those four years, righting the Burgundy and Gold's off-kilter ship, Gibbs knew in his heart that it was time for him to sail back to North Carolina, where his family had remained after he returned to coaching.

"The way we played in those last four games of the season [all victories]; I thought we had a great chance," Gibbs said during a press conference. "All of us were totally devoted to giving ourselves the best chance to go all the way. I felt like that was a real possibility. The

Seahawk game obviously was a shock for all of us. None of us liked the way that happened."

Following a team meeting the next day, Gibbs went to his home in North Carolina and had another meeting. This one was with his wife, Pat, his sons, J.D. and Coy, and the rest of his family.

"When I started back to D.C., I kind of had a real strong feeling in my heart of what I felt like I should do," said Gibbs. "So much of our life, Pat and the kids, as we grew up here and they grew up here; this is where we wanted to be. I felt like also another part of me [should be] with the family and everything there in Charlotte. I think everybody here is aware of the fact that [since] I came here four years ago, my family situation has dramatically changed [because of a grandson being diagnosed with leukemia]. Having gone through that change [and knowing the only way I can do] this job is going after it night and day. [Family] is something you think about all the time.

"I have always said that the most important thing I am going to leave on this earth, Pat and I, are going to be our kids, our grandkids, and the influence you have on others. My family situation being what it is right now, I told [Redskins owner Daniel Snyder] that I just did not feel like I could make the kind of commitment that I needed to make going forward this year knowing what my family situation was. I felt like they needed me."

The Redskins were 30–34 during Gibbs' second tour, and 1–2 in the postseason.

chapter 2

Coachspeak

George Allen, 1971–1977

"We knew that he was a player's coach and he was extremely respectful, particularly of the older players. He valued our opinions. George Allen brought an atmosphere of confidence [with him from coaching the Los Angeles Rams]. He brought with him, 'The defense is the side of the ball that wins games.' Many of the players that came with him—Jack Pardee, Myron Pottios—these guys were defensive players who believed that the defense was just as important as or more important than the offense. And that we could make the difference in a game.

"We all knew that we probably couldn't break 15-flat in the 100, but as a team working together, we made few, if any, mistakes. We could overcome virtually any other team and even dominate a lot of teams. And then of course, we knew, too, that scoring on defense is demoralizing to the other team. That was our goal in every game, to get one or two scores. These things led to a pride in ourselves with a dependency on our teammates."

—Mike Bass, cornerback

·

"[Having a third head coach in three years] didn't bother me. The big adjustment one has to make, especially if you're on offense and you've been coached by head coaches who have been basically offensive coaches, then there's where the adjustment has to be made. You've got a defensive-minded coach now who thinks the defense can score more points than the offense can.

"We took advantage of the talent we had and put points on the board. So it didn't change our focus or thought process in terms of how we performed. It did create a situation which probably the way some defensive players may have felt when you're coached by a head coach who has a basically offensive coaching background. You've got a situation where you've got two kids and the defensive team will be the favorite child rather than the offense for the first time in your life."

—Larry Brown, running back

•

"[After starting every game at defensive tackle as a rookie in 1970] they named Allen coach, and I knew of his reputation for [preferring to play seasoned veterans]. I'd just bought a house, the first house I ever bought in my life, and I don't know if I'm going to be on the team. So Allen called me up and said, 'I need to see you.' He said, 'You know, Bill, I was watching film of you and I'm going to move you to defensive end. It's your position to lose. We can build this defense around you.'

"About a month later, he has a press conference and says, 'I've never played rookies. That's not my style. I like veterans, and no rookie is ever going to play for me.' And so just before training camp, he pulls me in again. He says, 'Bill, I've been thinking about you. Even though you started all last year, I think the best thing for me to do is treat you just like a rookie.' Of course, they had traded for Verlon Biggs and Ron McDole. So that was the end of my having a locked-up defensive end job. That's the way George was. George would say things that he really believed at the time, but the statement quickly became inoperative."

—Bill Brundige, defensive lineman

•

"George was a very truthful, straightforward guy. He would tell you something and then turn around and tell someone else the exact same thing. He didn't pull any punches. What he would say to you, he'd say

George Allen guided the Redskins to Super Bowl VII in 1973, where they lost to the undefeated Miami Dolphins.

to the press or anybody else. Whereas some of the other coaches I played for didn't do that."

—Dave Butz, defensive tackle

•

"[When George Allen became my fourth head coach in four seasons, I sensed some stability] only because he surrounded me with old guys. You had to be suspicious, too. You look around, and the general feeling was you needed younger players. And he did keep some around, but he did create a different attitude, and he reached down to really deal with your desire to win. And he reminded us at the same time that our careers were at the threshold where it should be ending. He was a master of motivating people and reminding people of the value of playing together as a team. And he sold that idea!"

—Pat Fischer, cornerback

•

"We knew that he was defensive-oriented and he wanted a very conservative approach to offense [when he came to Washington in 1971]. But it really wasn't that conservative. He was going to take advantage of whatever a defense would allow him to do offensively. He just wanted mistake-free football on offense, defense, and special teams.

"He was the first coach that I'd had that really had a very comprehensive defensive system. Everybody else that I had played for up to that point, we really didn't have an arsenal to work out of like Coach Allen brought here."

—Chris Hanburger, linebacker

•

"He followed after Bill Austin had it in '70, after Lombardi died. Allen comes in and Allen was strictly a defensive coach. He wanted to win 7–3. Just don't make mistakes offensively, and we'll win defensively. That was his philosophy. And that was completely different from the way I had played.

"And Lombardi, being an offensive-minded coach, we had a lot of weapons and we just didn't use them. [Allen] changed all the keys in the passing game. The things that we did were just backwards for me and it just didn't work."

—Sonny Jurgensen, quarterback

•

"In those days, I think the draft was either late January or early February, and we rushed in [to Washington] in early January [1971] ourselves and we were staying at a downtown hotel and getting ready for the draft.

"I remember the morning of the draft, George Allen asked me to meet him down in the lobby of the hotel and we'd walk over together. As we left, the doorman said to George, 'I hope you have a good draft.' He said, 'We're going to have the best draft we ever had.' He didn't say anything more to me.

"When we got to the Redskins facility, he called a meeting [with the assistant coaches] and said, 'Fellas, about 4:00 this morning, I concluded a trade. I traded with the L.A. Rams.' And then he gave a litany of names: John Wilbur, Jeff Jordan, Diron Talbert, Myron Pottios, Maxie Baughan, Jack Pardee, and Richie Petitbon. We sat there stunned. And then finally one of our coaches said, 'What did we give?' He said, 'Our first, second, third, fourth, and fifth draft choices this year and next.' [Actually, they gave up Marlin McKeever, the first and third picks in 1971, and the third, fourth, fifth, sixth, and seventh picks in 1972.]

"George, I think, traded away 20-some draft choices before the beginning of that year and brought in a lot of fine players. Ron McDole from Buffalo, Verlon Biggs from the Jets, Billy Kilmer. We came in with a great deal of optimism. I had great faith in George. I thought he brought in an outstanding staff. Guys like Ted Marchibroda, Mike McCormack. So we were encouraged. We came in with very positive feelings."

—Marv Levy, assistant coach

•

"I loved him. Even though it was just for one year, to play for a coach like that, especially as a defensive player, was really, really a great opportunity. He was definitely a player's coach. He'd do whatever the players wanted. He'd work you hard and was a real stickler to make sure that mentally, everybody knew exactly what was going to take place. Not only playing for a coach like that, but with so many veterans, was really great for my career."

—Mark Murphy, safety

•

"I had retired from professional football because I was tired of losing and I didn't think the [Rams'] coaching situation [prior to Allen] was putting the effort into winning that should be put. So I retired and went back to play with George. Actually, I played eight years and retired and came back and played seven more with him.

"His dedication to winning, the way he treated the players, what he expected.... He expected to win! We worked long, but it was still good for an old player to play for him."

—Jack Pardee, linebacker

Joe Gibbs, 1981–1992, 2004–2007

"I don't think you ever know what you've got until it actually gets there. In '81 he did what many new coaches do. He came in and really cleaned house, [getting rid of] a lot of the remnants of the 1980 team from the Over-the-Hill Gang. You had a lot of guys from the George Allen era, and he really got rid of a lot of them.

"He tried to implement that 'Air Coryell' offense. He got [running back John] Riggins back from his one-year sabbatical. And after five games, we were 0–5, and I think he realized that he needed to fit the offense to the personnel as opposed to tying the offense to who's ever out there. Instead of throwing the ball 55 times a game, we started running it 55 times a game."

—Jeff Bostic, center

•

"Coach Gibbs was a great coach. He knew how to motivate, he knew how to win, and he had great schemes. [Richie] Petitbon and [Larry] Peccatiello, those guys were very good [assistant] coaches, and they had some very good ballplayers. Gibbs knew how to win at the end. You could go into halftime close, and he'd make the adjustments. You never want to sit and get beat by something that's not working. The coaches were very smart."

—Todd Bowles, safety

•

"A great offensive mind! I'd give him a 98 as far as coaching ability. I'm not going to give anybody a 100. But he definitely deserves a 100, for sure. I would give him a 100 for aligning his assistant coaches around him. I think that was the biggest difference."

—Monte Coleman, linebacker

•

"We had outstanding leadership starting with Joe Gibbs. He believed in his players, and the players believed in him. He made us feel like we could beat anybody. We were a team that didn't have a whole bunch of stars early on and eventually we started getting some additional players who ultimately became stars, but they didn't think they were stars. They just said, 'Okay, I'm playing pretty good.' They didn't think they were, as Joe Gibbs would say, 'the best thing since sliced bread.'"

—Vernon Dean, cornerback

•

"Everybody contributed to what we were doing. We were all on the same page, we all communicated with each other, and we knew what we were there to do. Everybody knew what their responsibility was, and we knew what we had to do to get it done.

"And we had a great leader in Joe Gibbs. I think the way he operates the system, he built everything on the foundation of family. He wasn't afraid to delegate authority to his [assistant] coaches. He was like, 'Do what you do best, and we'll work it from there.' He didn't have a lot of rules and regulations. He basically said, 'Hey, just use common sense. If you don't have common sense, you probably won't be here.'

"You respected him. He has a captivating presence. When he stands in front of a room—without screaming and yelling—he can bring you to the point where you're ready to just go out and do whatever you need to do to get it done."

—Darryl Grant, defensive tackle

•

"He just instilled in us to be the best team that we can be. Back then, you didn't have the salary cap and free agency like you have now. It was more of team camaraderie. Basically, the nucleus was the same group of people, and that's why I think it was so great. We had the same leaders on the team, and everybody worked well together. The team chemistry was great, and you have to credit Joe Gibbs for having a perfect mix.

"I was a 10th-round draft choice [in 1984] and I remember there was another running back that they drafted, Jimmy Smith, and he was drafted in the fourth round, and I'm the one that ended up staying on the team [longer than that one season]. A lot of teams would say we spent X amount of money on this guy. They didn't look at it like that. They took the best people no matter where you were drafted. It's what you could contribute to the team. They did a great job with that, and I think that's what made them so good during those years."

—Keith Griffin, running back

•

"I think Joe Gibbs was so successful because he had a direct line to God. This man had a faith that was unshakable. He was a fair man. He was a good man. One thing I liked about Joe Gibbs, you see a lot of coaches, they do a lot of ranting and raving, they embarrass players on the field. Joe Gibbs would never embarrass a player publicly. If you did something or didn't do your job, he'd call you into the office and sit down and talk with you. He'd treat you like a man. He'd give you a chance to sort of succeed or fail.

"I had a learning disability, and that whole coaching staff had a lot of tolerance with me. They sort of treated me with kid gloves. They kept encouraging me, 'Hey, you know the plays.' And even when I didn't know the plays, they kept me on that football field. And so that's what I liked about Joe Gibbs.

"Plus, he had a heart for all kinds of people: the poor and the sick and the suffering addicts, alcoholics who were out there. He'd started taking me when I was a rookie, going to these sorts of halfway houses talking to these kids. Here was this white guy going to this black community and sitting there talking to them about the Lord and the Bible and reading Bible verses with them. So I had a lot of respect for him and I felt like he brought me along to be sort of like a father figure and sort of show me the way. He was just a different kind of guy."

—Dexter Manley, defensive end

.

"I think he was fair. He treated everybody the same way. He was a straight shooter. And I would say the thing about Coach Gibbs, he basically told me they were going to allow me a year to learn my trade because they were changing me from quarterback to another position [and] then I could battle for a job. He told me the more things I could do, the longer I could play, and I took heed to that. I tried to do as many positions as I can, as good as I can, and it kept me around for 14 years.

"And the one thing that made him a lot better than most coaches, he knew how to adjust. Many coaches put a game plan in during the week and they feel like they're married to it, they can't change. Coach Gibbs would put in a game plan; we'll go the first half, and if it didn't work, he'll come in for the second half and he'll tear it up and he'll say this is what we're going to run. We always had those go-to plays. His halftime adjustments I think were the greatest. I don't think I played for a coach that was better than him."

—Brian Mitchell, running back

.

"He was really a player's coach. He was innovative with a lot of stuff, like in training camp, he started us weightlifting. It wasn't all just hit, hit, hit, trying to wear everybody down. He was smart enough to know by that time pretty much who were the hitters and who weren't. He used his head on a lot of things, his gut, as he always said. We were a tough team, but yet we didn't do unnecessary stuff."

—Neal Olkewicz, linebacker

.

"I really didn't talk to him all that much. My thing was basically to not make waves and not be in trouble a lot. Just try to do what I was expected to do.

"But I think we had a good relationship. He knew where I stood, and I knew what he wanted as a player. He wanted somebody just to be consistent and not make a lot of errors, not make a lot of mistakes. Just perform hopefully to the best of my ability."

—Don Warren, tight end

Vince Lombardi, 1969

"I would probably give the credit [for being the team's first 1,000-yard rusher in 1970] to Vince Lombardi in this respect; I worked very hard that first year [1969] to win his confidence and the right to start at the running back position.

"The first game in 1969 [at New Orleans], I did not start the first half. He started the veterans. It was probably the best thing to do, to give the veterans a shot to keep their positions. But they didn't do extremely well, so he yanked them out and put myself and [fullback] Charley Harraway in.

"My first running play, I didn't particularly carry out that assignment very well. And then with some increasing pressure from him on the sideline, I began to develop some sort of rhythm in the way I was running. He had this rule that you stay with the [assigned blocking] hole. I'm saying to myself, 'This guy's crazy! There is no hole!' So I had to find holes. He said, 'Fine, you have broken a rule. But every time you deviate from the rule, you'd better not come up with losing yardage.' I guess because of the fear that I had being confronted by him, I was even more determined to find what you'd call 'daylight' if it wasn't where it was supposed to be. That meant you had to think quicker and you had to move quicker. That helped me develop a kind of rhythm that I needed to be a good running back in the National Football League."

—Larry Brown, running back

•

"He was a lot more than a coach. He taught you a lot about life as well as football. And of course, he brought with him quite a history. You were really in awe of him in everything that he did and said. He was just a wonderful person to be around despite all the supposedly bad things that you heard about him, how he could be and so on. But I found him to be a remarkable human being."

—Chris Hanburger, linebacker

•

"Of the nine different head coaches that I had, he was head and shoulders above everybody else. No comparison. It was easy to see why Green Bay was so successful. Of all the coaches I played for, he simplified the game instead of trying to complicate it. If I could have played my career with him, it would have made the game a lot of fun."

—Sonny Jurgensen, quarterback

Legendary head coach Vince Lombardi guided the 1969 Redskins to a 7–5–2 record, their first winning season in 14 years.

"He scared us into a winning season. We were the same team that had won only five of 14 games in 1968. In 1969 we were 7–5–2, a big turn-around.

"Lombardi was determined to make us into the Green Bay Packers. But we had different personnel. We were a much faster team. We had Charley Taylor by then, and Larry Brown, and Sonny Jurgensen had the quick release. He spent most of the training camp getting us to run the 'Lombardi Sweep,' but we were too fast for it. Our timing was always off and we couldn't slow down to make the cuts.

"Green Bay was a precision team. It was perfect for them with Paul Hornung and Jim Taylor, but not right for us. By the end of training camp, Coach Lombardi realized that. I remember he said to me, 'I made a mistake. We've got to do it differently.' We did, and it worked."

—Bobby Mitchell, receiver

Bill McPeak, 1961–1965

"Bill McPeak was a very good head coach. I liked Bill McPeak. He had some inexperienced coaches. Ted Marchibroda was just starting, that was his first year. I used to tell him, 'If you surround yourself with incompetent people, they're going to take you down.' And that's what happened to him. I liked him as a coach. He was a nice man."

—Sonny Jurgensen, quarterback

•

"I really thought a lot of Bill, what he did for me. He was primarily a defensive player and then a defensive coach and he really gave me a tremendous understanding of defense. That helped me more than anything through my career because of that factor: how to recognize the tips, what the purposes of the defenses were, and all that."

—Norm Snead, quarterback

Jack Pardee, 1978–1980

"Jack could definitely coach. He was a very good coach! He was good for me because Jack was a linebacker and [had] a defensive mind that had a good scheme. If I was going to put a question mark on him or his coaching abilities, I'd give him a 95. As far as aligning himself up with assistant coaches, I'd give him an 80."

—Monte Coleman, linebacker

.

"It was tough for all of us [former teammates] that were still here when he became the [head] coach [in 1978]. I think it was even difficult for Jack. He may never admit that, but I personally think it was very difficult for him. As I look back on it, I think he probably, at least I would hope that he would admit that it did affect how he did things. I don't think he wanted to, whether it was right or wrong, really get too close to the players that he had played with, and I think that was a big mistake. That's my personal feeling."

—Chris Hanburger, linebacker

.

"Yeah, in a way [I thought it was difficult to play for a former teammate]. I think the problem was that Jack was the [head] coach and they brought [Bobby] Beathard in as the general manager. Of course, Beathard wanted to build the team, his team, which is what you're supposed to do. I know Jack tried to do both. He tried to pacify playing younger guys and this type of thing, where we were so used to George [Allen], where he did everything to win that week and we'd worry about next week later.

"So we started playing some people that just weren't ready to play. And also, defensively, we had to curtail it a lot. For example, we never really ran the huddle call. We'd probably run it 10 percent of the time. So everything was automatic all the way around. What we really did was outsmart people. We'd get in defenses so they couldn't dictate. Most of the time, they'd come out and set up in a formation and it would kind of dictate what defense you'd get. With George, we'd have three or four different defenses for every formation so they couldn't do that. And then we'd have a lot of individual check-offs that we could run. And we couldn't do that anymore.

"We had to get real simple. And when we got real simple, that hurt the older guys. It took the advantage away that we had. In other words, we had to line up and play a simple defense, and that made it very difficult for some players. We lost the advantage of being able to outsmart people, and it caught up with us. We won the first five or six games and then we never won another one."

—Ron McDole, defensive end

•

"Jack kind of inherited the team that George [Allen] had. It's not a situation where you just win a Super Bowl. It takes some years of working together to put a Super Bowl team together, and Jack did that. He continued what George was doing. He was able to mold Joe Theismann, John Riggins, Dave Butz, and some of the Hogs.

"Jack actually did a good job in my opinion. He kind of molded those Super Bowl teams that came up. He has to get some of the credit for being able to train those guys. You've got to train players. You've got to train quarterbacks. You've got to train defensive linemen. You've got to train the team concept, teach guys to pull together. So I would say that Jack deserves some credit for those Super Bowl teams even though they fired him."

—Diron Talbert, defensive tackle

pick up the ball and that it would slip out of his hand as he attempted to pass. But it did, and I was right there to nail him when the ball popped up in the air. And really, it was just me and him there, and he's 5'4", 5'6" and I'm 6', so I just went up after the ball."

Having out-rebounded his former teammate, Bass' attention quickly focused on not letting the turnover become a personal embarrassment.

"All I could think about when I caught the ball was, 'I can't let Garo tackle me. I can't let [the holder and veteran quarterback] Earl Morrall tackle me.' I'd never hear the end of it," laughed Bass. "When I got past those two guys, I thought, as I was going into the end zone, that we've got a chance now to win this game. I knew that our offense could score two touchdowns. Unfortunately, it didn't work out that way.

"I wear this NFC championship ring—I call it the 'loser's ring in the Super Bowl.' But so many people when I say that have said, 'Well, there are a lot of players who never, ever get to the Super Bowl.' And as the years go by, I appreciate it more and more. I consider myself lucky."

Jeff Bostic

Sure, many football fans are aware that the Redskins won three Super Bowls with three different quarterbacks under center. But how many realize that the center for each one of Washington's championships was Jeff Bostic?

During the first victory, Super Bowl XVII over Miami, he snapped the ball to Joe Theismann and realized a lifelong dream.

"I remember going on the field, and I don't know that my feet hit the ground the first three or four plays. The whole warm-up, the first three or four plays and then you kind of get whacked and say, 'This is a game!'" laughed Bostic. "The experience was phenomenal.

"That was one of the good things about it being a strike-shortened season. After the NFC Championship Game, [instead of the normal two-week gap] the next week was the Super Bowl. We didn't have time to get caught up in all the hoopla. We were young enough that we didn't know to be scared."

chapter 3

Super Bowl Sunday

Mike Bass

It's unusual for the same play to be a highlight and also be prominently in an NFL Films' follies production. However, tha occurred during Washington's Super Bowl VII game against M Los Angeles' Memorial Coliseum.

With the goal to cap off the league's first and only perfect sea leading 14–0 with just over two minutes remaining in the quarter, the Dolphins sent kicker Garo Yepremian into the attempt a 42-yard field goal. As a result of a bad snap, Yepremia himself with the ball and sauntering toward the sideline with t and deftness of a newborn colt attempting its first steps.

Surprisingly, however, that was not the least graceful part of Under pressure, Yepremian decided to attempt a pass, which wa by Washington's Mike Bass. And with what was officially a fuml ery, the veteran cornerback returned the ball 49 yards to the enc the only Redskins touchdown in the 14–7 loss.

"Garo and I had been teammates in Detroit. We had both the taxi squad, so we had known each other since 1967. My j special teams was to be what you call the 'spy man,'" said Bas event that there was a kick attempt that was blocked, my job wa ally be there to pick up the ball. And there was a block that I and ran for a touchdown against the Cardinals, so I knew tha happen.

"I always anticipated that there was going to be a block came in the Super Bowl, I was ready, but I didn't expect that G

The Redskins in the Super Bowl

Super Bowl VII   Miami Dolphins 14, Redskins 7
January 14, 1973   Memorial Coliseum—Los Angeles, California

Super Bowl XVII   Redskins 27, Miami Dolphins 17
January 30, 1983   Rose Bowl—Pasadena, California

Super Bowl XVIII   Los Angeles Raiders 38, Redskins 9
January 22, 1984   Tampa Stadium—Tampa, Florida

Super Bowl XXII   Redskins 42, Denver Broncos 10
January 31, 1988   Jack Murphy Stadium—San Diego, California

Super Bowl XXVI   Redskins 37, Buffalo Bills 24
January 26, 1992   Hubert H. Humphrey Metrodome—Minneapolis, Minnesota

They were certainly less scared when the Redskins won Super Bowl XXII over Denver with Doug Williams calling signals, or when they captured Super Bowl XXVI away from Buffalo with Mark Rypien leading the offense. Winning the three Lombardi Trophies in 10 years are incredibly special memories for Bostic. But he finds the Super Bowl XVIII loss to the Raiders to be just as unforgettable.

"I'm convinced that if we had won against the Raiders, that would have been considered one of the greatest teams in the [history of the] league," Bostic said. "We set the scoring record with 541 points. We were 16–2 going into that game, and we lost the two games by one point!

"[Super Bowl XVIII] was a horrible experience. You couldn't get in and out of the hotel. Our practice facility was probably 35, 40 minutes from our hotel, and it was right along the highway. I'm convinced [Raiders owner] Al Davis had somebody watching our practices. And then we get to the game, and it's like Murphy's Law. Whatever could go wrong, did go wrong. But you've got to give credit to the Raiders. They played great. I think that had the potential to be a great game if we'd shown up."

Perry Brooks

Defensive tackle Perry Brooks may have had a broken leg when the Redskins met Miami in Super Bowl XVII, but he wasn't going to let that keep him off the field, much less hinder the event.

"It was exciting to see all those people in the Rose Bowl, 100,000-plus," Brooks said, "and getting an opportunity for the whole world to see you, millions of people all over the world, from here to Hong Kong to Africa. And to see your fans in the stadium, to see the burgundy and gold there, playing for the world title and becoming champions—it was a great, great experience."

While the 27–17 victory over the Dolphins may have been a great experience, the 38–9 loss to the then–Los Angeles Raiders in Super Bowl XVIII a year later was definitely not.

"You sit back and think about what caused this and what caused that, but I don't think it was overconfidence. I just think it wasn't our day," said Brooks. "To go into the Super Bowl and have the first punt blocked against you, you don't know what play it takes to turn a ball-game around. When something's never happened to you before, it sort of has a mental effect on you. Then you start trying so hard, and before you know anything, you make another mistake in a crucial situation.

"Before you know anything, you're down 14–0 and playing against a high-caliber team like the Raiders were at that time. You can't give a wounded dog any kind of ammunition. You give him too much raw meat; sooner or later he might come back and bite you.

"So that's what happened. Going into halftime, [Redskins quarterback] Joe Theismann threw a ball up, and it was grabbed by [Raiders linebacker] Jack Squirek. He ran it in for a touchdown, and before you know anything, we go into halftime down 21–3 instead of 14–3 and still in the game. It's hard to come back from that. Everybody in the world knows that you ain't going to run the ball, and we happened to be a running team. They knew you were going to throw. They knew exactly what you were going to do."

Larry Brown

Larry Brown's efforts during the 1972 campaign resulted in his leading the conference in rushing despite missing two games because of injuries. He had a team-record 1,216 yards, averaging 4.3 yards per carry, and was named as the NFL's Player of the Year.

The Miami Dolphins, however, proved to be the team of the year during Super Bowl VII. The perfect team, if you will. Arriving on Super Sunday with a perfect record, they held Washington's offense scoreless in the 14–7 victory and limited Brown to just 72 yards on 22 carries, a 3.3 average.

"In retrospect, I know what happened," said Brown. "I've had an opportunity to talk to a number of the defensive players on the Dolphins since then. I think that we just got outplayed and probably outcoached. Especially from a defensive standpoint.

"[Miami's] defensive people were told to not pay a great deal of attention to [quarterback] Billy Kilmer's ability to pass. Concentrate on me. Do not take lanes, just make contact and hold ground. Do not take a right move or a left move in a lane—just wait!"

Brown continued. "So therefore, there weren't any holes. The lanes were clogged up with those big bodies. Once the original hole was closed, there were no other opportunities. That's why I took so much of a pounding. At some point in time you say there's nothing there and you just put your head down and go on up in there. Of course, they wouldn't have been able to do that if [an injured] Sonny [Jurgensen] had started the game [at quarterback]. I'm not sure whether Sonny was able to play or not."

Bill Brundige

After destroying Dallas in the 1972 NFC Championship Game, 26–3, to win their first championship in 30 years, the Redskins had another date with history in Super Bowl VII. The AFC champion Miami Dolphins were undefeated and looking to add an exclamation point to their perfect season.

Washington's defensive lineman Bill Brundige felt that he and his teammates were just looking to get back on the field and that the two weeks between the postseason games were anything but perfect.

"Every day you had two hours set aside for the media and you couldn't do anything but sit there on the field to wait to be interviewed. Well, that was fine for Sonny Jurgensen, Billy Kilmer, and Larry Brown. But for us peons, my local paper or the *Denver Post* may want to talk to me," says the Colorado native, "but the rest of the time we just sat there and did nothing. It was such a circus that we just completely lost focus on the game."

As the boredom and interviews were getting closer to being replaced by blocking and interceptions, the Redskins' attention focused more on the Dolphins.

"We were not impressed with Miami," Brundige said. "They, I don't think, had really beaten anybody that was a great team during the season. Their two playoff victories were very, very close games. And, frankly, going into the game, I didn't think that there's any way we could lose."

So much for his being a prophet. The Dolphins won, 14–7. But what wasn't predicted was that Brundige would be directly involved with Washington's side of the scoreboard. Albeit with a little help from a Cyprus-born kicker who didn't exactly have a finely tuned passing touch.

Looking to increase its lead in the fourth quarter, Miami sent Garo Yepremian in to try a 42-yard field goal. But after Brundige broke through the line of scrimmage and blocked the kick, Yepremian picked up the ball, ran to his right, and tried what one would be hard-pressed to label a pass attempt. Brundige tipped the airborne fumble into the hands of his teammate Mike Bass, who returned it 49 yards for a touchdown.

"The real story is that Bob Heinz was trying to block me, and [he's] 6′6″. So I stood him up and put my hand up. The ball never hit me! It hit him on the back of the head!" said Brundige. "And then I started chasing Yepremian around. He's left-handed and tried to throw the ball right-handed. I was bearing down on him and I was so exhausted, it was 87 degrees that day, and my tongue was hanging out. I probably looked like I was trying to kill him when all I was trying to do was survive.

"So when he went to throw the ball, it squirted out of his hand and actually went backwards. Mike Bass caught it in midair. I'm running down the sideline and I trip and fall down, and [Dolphins quarterback Earl] Morrall falls over me.

"They had a sequence [of photos the following day] on the front page of the *Los Angeles Times* that said, 'Bill Brundige blocks field goal.' And then it said, 'Bill Brundige tips a pass.' And then it shows that Morrall is the last guy between Mike Bass and a touchdown, and it shows me throwing a block. My mother bought about 50 copies of the paper."

Dave Butz

Defensive tackle Dave Butz was in his 10th season and had experienced playing in just one playoff game when, instead of watching a Super Bowl game from his living room couch, he got to witness the league's championship game through his face mask.

The Redskins went 8–1 during the strike-shortened 1982 season and beat Miami in Super Bowl XVII, 27–17.

Washington represented the NFC in Super Bowl XVIII a year later, but fell to the then–Los Angeles Raiders, 38–9.

An opportunity for redemption came four seasons later in Super Bowl XXII, and the Redskins took home the Lombardi Trophy after dumping Denver 42–10.

Three Super Bowls: two victories, one loss, and only one man wearing the burgundy and gold's No. 65 jersey.

"All three of them were different," said Butz, No. 65. "The thing that struck me was that years later I talked with some of the [assistant] coaches, and they said, 'We knew that we'd win the Super Bowl.' I said, 'How did you know that?' And they said, 'Because each and every guy did his own coaching. Everybody watched enough film and saw stuff on players.'

"It's kind of disappointing after you win because there's nobody left to play. It just totally shuts off. It's like slamming into a brick wall at 50 miles per hour. Everybody's fine tuned. Everybody knows their own job. Everybody's on the same page and knows what has to be accomplished. You can't have any fishes swimming upstream or against the system. I don't care how many millions they're paid, if they don't believe in the system, you need to get rid of them because it's like a cancer. And we had none of that when we won the Super Bowls."

Butz has memories of the Super Bowl loss to the Raiders, as well. "That was the first time in my life that I ever got beat up in a game," said the 6′8″, 320-pound team captain. "A friend of mine parked the car on the other side of the stadium grounds, and I can remember going to the car and stopping to rest because I was in such pain."

Earnest Byner

Postseason games didn't monopolize Earnest Byner's list of fondest football memories. A fumble at the 3-yard line as he, then with the Cleveland Browns, was going for a game-tying touchdown with just over a minute left on the clock in the AFC Championship Game against Denver on January 17, 1988, will do that. However, in 1991 the running back played well enough to not only start a new list, but do so using a Sharpie.

He rushed for team-high 1,048 yards as the Redskins advanced to Super Bowl XXVI against Buffalo. And with a 10-yard touchdown reception from Mark Rypien, he not only helped Washington win the title, 37–24, he won a personal battle, as well.

"My greatest experience was actually winning the NFC Championship Game [vs. Detroit]," Byner laughed. "I cried almost all the way to the stadium and even cried when I was playing because I was so emotionally charged for that game. So an opportunity to finally get past that plateau that I had been on as far as championship games...."

"Playing in the Super Bowl was actually a little bit more subdued until the first play. I ran the ball and got swamped by Buffalo's defense. And right there for an instant, I thought, 'Gosh, the whole world is watching.' And that was a magnificent feeling. After that, the game was on. Catching the first touchdown for our team, winning the Super Bowl was a dream come true."

Byner continued. "That whole season was really a dream. I think it was a culmination of the experience that Coach Gibbs had had over the years, the respect he had for the veteran players, and the relationship he had established. The overall chemistry of that team was somewhat spirited. It was a genuine caring for one another. All those combined produced a magical year."

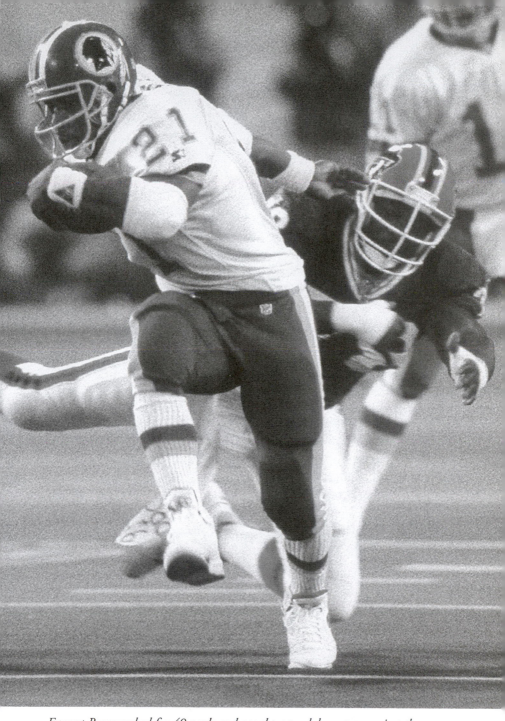

Earnest Byner rushed for 49 yards and caught a touchdown pass against the Buffalo Bills in Super Bowl XXVI.

Ken Coffey

In what was about as close as you could get to a dress rehearsal in the NFL, rookie safety Ken Coffey traveled to Super Bowl XVII as a member of Washington's injured reserve list.

"That was fantastic! That was as fun a time as I had not playing football, but being involved in," Coffey said of the Redskins' title game versus Miami. "The backdrop is that the Super Bowl was in Los Angeles. And one of the things I love about this country is we see a need and we do a good job filling the need. And occasionally, when there isn't a need, we go out and we create one. They've overblown this championship football game into an event. I mean, the game [now] is almost an afterthought.

"But being able to go out there and not have to worry about playing and just experience it, we had a wonderful time. I practiced hard doing the scout team stuff. I got to go out and meet a lot of people and see a lot of things. It was just a good deal."

The following season, as a player on the active roster, the Super Bowl XVIII result wasn't such a good deal for Coffey and his teammates. The Redskins were beaten by the Raiders, 38–9.

"[For the previous Super Bowl] we were staying in a nice Westin in Costa Mesa, and [this Super Bowl] was in Tampa. And Tampa was not then what it is now. We lost the coin toss and the bus ended up pulling in front of a Holiday Inn. That's when I knew we were in trouble," laughed Coffey. "You go from a Westin to a Holiday Inn. And I don't care what type of Holiday Inn it is; it's still a Holiday Inn.

"I always thought that I would be back there. Whereas I enjoyed it and was thankful for it, I didn't realize—and this is what a lot of the older players will also tell you—there are a lot of guys who don't experience this once, much less twice. On one hand, it was good not to be overawed by it, but on the other hand, there really is a sense that it's very fleeting and you should enjoy it for all it's worth."

Monte Coleman

Beginning in 1979, Monte Coleman was with the Redskins for three seasons, winning 24 games and losing 24 games, before the memorable

1982 campaign broke the deadlock. Compiling an 8–1 record during the strike-shortened season, he and his teammates won the NFC championship and advanced to Super Bowl XVII, where they beat the Miami Dolphins, 27–17.

"I didn't know what to expect," said Coleman. "There was nobody on the team at that time that had ever gone to the Super Bowl. It was pretty much a business trip. The glamour side of it and all that, took care of itself after the game. But that was bigger than life to be able to play in the Super Bowl. It was a dream come true."

The following season: same dream, different conclusion. The Redskins posted a 14–2 mark, captured the conference title again, but were bamboozled by the Raiders in Super Bowl XVIII, 38–9.

"The Raiders were a better team that day, and I think we were a little overconfident," Coleman said. "I think that team was the best team we had throughout my [16-year] career.

"If you remember, [earlier that season, on October 2], we beat the Raiders in RFK [37–35] in a last-minute heroic catch by Joe Washington. The year before was a strike year, and we had one week to prepare for the Super Bowl [following the NFC Championship Game]. This year, we had two weeks to prepare for the Super Bowl. I think the extra week kind of hurt us.

"We were underdogs in the first Super Bowl and we were actually favorites against the Raiders. And that's the one we stunk it up in."

Coleman would play in two other odor-free Super Bowls for the Redskins—both victories—Super Bowl XXII versus Denver and Super Bowl XXVI against the Buffalo Bills.

Andre Collins

Following a season that saw him start every game and tie Dexter Manley's team rookie record with six sacks, left outside linebacker Andre Collins switched with Wilber Marshall in 1991 and lined up at the right, or weak-side, linebacker position.

"It didn't really mean a whole lot in the scheme of our defense," said Collins. "It's just that Wilber was a bigger, more physical player than I was. A lot of the teams were trying to take advantage of my lightness, I'll call it. So we stuck Wilber over there, and he was a little tougher than I was against the run, and that made our team better. I was able to go on the weak side and use my speed and chase plays from the backside and to cover backs. It just worked out."

In fact, it worked out very well. After three consecutive seasons of finishing third in the division to the New York Giants and Philadelphia, the Redskins compiled an NFL-best 14–2 record. What was the key to their success?

"It was just a bunch of veteran players that had a history of winning a lot of games," Collins said. "I'm talking about Joe Jacoby, Russ Grimm, Jim Lachey, Earnest Byner, Gerald Riggs, Art Monk, Ricky Sanders, Gary Clark, and that's just offense. These guys knew how to put points on the board, and that made our job easy.

"We opened the season with a 45–0 win over Detroit, and that's just amazing. It just made the defense's job a lot easier, and we had some beef up front ourselves with Charles Mann, a young Bobby Wilson, Fred Stokes, and Markus Koch. We had big people up front offensively and defensively, and that just allowed us to really muscle a lot of the teams that we played."

That includes the 41–10 victory over Detroit in the NFC Championship Game, and beating the Buffalo Bills in Super Bowl XXVI, 37–24.

"I probably didn't fully appreciate it the way that I would have at the end of my career. That Super Bowl was so amazing I just assumed I was going to the playoffs and going to the Super Bowl just about every year, and that never really happened," said Collins, who would spend five seasons in Washington. "Looking back, I remember being relieved that we won because we had been the best team all year. And I remember the season getting long and there was more and more pressure to win and win big! When we finally won the Super Bowl, it was nice to say, 'Okay, we were the best team in football all year. We finally did it.'

"Looking back, I would have loved to have appreciated it probably like a Monte Coleman or a Wilber Marshall. I remember those guys being elated and me, just a young, dumb kid. I was like, 'Whoop-de-do, it's just another championship.'"

Vernon Dean

Many players toil for years in the NFL and about as close as they come to getting to a Super Bowl is watching it on television. Vernon Dean actually made it to the league championship game in less than a typical season. Twelve games to be exact.

Washington's top draft choice in 1982, the rookie cornerback experienced a 57-day players' strike after playing in just two games and then helped his teammates put up an 8–1 record in the shortened season.

"I really didn't know what to think because it was an argument that had been going on prior to me getting there," said Dean. "I was informed that there could possibly be a strike, but I didn't know what to think other than to follow the veterans. I really didn't understand what was going on. I didn't understand the labor agreement and all that stuff. I learned as I went along."

Once the labor issues were settled and the players traded picket signs for shoulder pads, Washington went through the playoffs with an attitude, outscoring its opponents 83–31.

"When we started winning, you just expected to win. As a rookie, I really didn't know anything differently. I was told the team that usually plays the best in December usually ends up going to the Super Bowl. And we were actually playing pretty good through the month of December. So I was once again following the veteran leadership."

Dean and the veterans played very well in January, too. Dropping the Dolphins in Super Bowl XVII, 27–17, the rookie felt fortunate that he was able to reach the ultimate in the profession so soon in his career.

"I didn't know what to expect," Dean said. "Other guys who had been around, some older veterans, to them, it was a relief because they had been in the league for 10 years and they'd never gone [to a Super Bowl]. So seeing their excitement made me understand and appreciate how fortunate I was."

Fortunately for the Redskins and their fans, the excitement carried over to the following season. Totaling five interceptions, Dean helped Washington win another NFC title and return to play on Super Sunday. That, however, is when the momentum came to an end. The Raiders won Super Bowl XVIII 38–9.

"I would say we felt good about our chances. I think we just kind of took things for granted and I think the Raiders came in a bit more focused. We had actually beaten them earlier that year, and I think they were just a little hungrier because everybody was talking about how we were the favorites. I'm not going to say we were overconfident. I think we just took a few things for granted. I don't think we focused like we had done in the past."

Clint Didier

From the day he was selected in the 12th round of the 1981 NFL Draft, it's highly doubtful anyone would have ever accused Clint Didier of taking anything for granted. Spending his first season on Washington's practice squad, about the only ones who knew his name were the other players on the practice squad. He was, however, on the roster the next year.

"I'll tell you what, it was close. It was nip and tuck," said Didier. "I was in contact with Wayne Sevier, who was the special-teams coach, and he was frank with me. He'd say, 'Hey, you're on the line, you're on the bubble, you'd better do something this week.'

"And so the pressure was on big time! Your job's never fully intact. When you're on the bubble like that, there's always the chance if someone became available and they need a position, you're gone. But the good Lord had his vision and his destiny for me, and thank God I had Joe Gibbs as a head coach. Because I think without the patience of that man, I'd have never seen the NFL." Much less be in uniform on Super Sunday at the end of the season. But when the Redskins took the field at the Rose Bowl for Super Bowl XVII against Miami, there was Didier.

"I never in my wildest dreams would ever think that my first year I played in the NFL, I would go to a Super Bowl and win it," Didier said of the 27–17 victory over the Dolphins. "There are guys that play long careers and never see a Super Bowl. And here I am, my first year, barely hanging on by the skin of my teeth."

A bit more secure the following season, Didier and his teammates returned to the league's title game and met the Raiders in Super Bowl XVIII. A team they had defeated earlier in the season, 37–35.

"We beat them, but we knew we had not beaten them soundly. We knew that was a good team," said Didier. "What I think was instrumental [prior to the Super Bowl] was all the hype during that week of practice, that the Raiders were doing everything they could to win the game. They caught people with cameras filming our practices. We were all aware of this.

"And then when we did get into the game, they were ready to play! You can almost tell when you go into a game whether your personnel, the players you're playing with, are physically, but more importantly, mentally ready to play a hard-nosed, tough game. And I don't think we were because they walked their linebackers up there and really hurt our running game. We couldn't get the edge [and fell to the Raiders 38–9]."

Ricky Ervins

Being a contributing rookie on a football team that compiles a 14–2 record, wins the NFC championship, and is heading to the Super Bowl could make a dream come true.

That, however, was not the case for running back Ricky Ervins in 1991. After helping the Redskins reach those accomplishments, the experience that was Super Bowl XXVI against Buffalo was not how he expected it would be at all.

"We never got a chance to experience the whole week. We had it in Minnesota, and there was nothing but snow there," laughed Ervins. "When you go to Super Bowls now when they have them in Miami or Pasadena, the whole week is a festivity of things going on. We never had that NFL experience.

"Once you get to the game and all the hoopla that's going on, the singers and the balloons inside the building, it hit me. That year, we were constantly winning, so I was used to winning. So when we played Buffalo, it was just another game. But once the game was over with and you see [video] tapes that they make up, that's when it hits you. Wow! I actually played in that game."

He certainly did. As the game's leading rusher with 72 yards on 13 carries, the rookie shined under the league's biggest spotlight.

"I don't think about that much. I just wish I could have scored a touchdown because they show the touchdowns on TV. They don't show the rushes," Ervins chuckled. "And I had a chance to get one. I got down to the goal line and they brought [Gerald] Riggs in. But hey, that was our game plan." And it was successful. Washington beat the Bills, 37–24.

Darryl Grant returned an interception for a touchdown in the 1982 NFC Championship Game against the Dallas Cowboys.

Darryl Grant

The 1982 season, Darryl Grant's second, was a whirlwind for him. He was shifted from the offensive line to defensive tackle during training camp. He moved into the starting lineup midway through the season after Perry Brooks was sidelined because of a broken leg.

And then during the NFC Championship Game against Dallas, he caught a Gary Hogeboom pass that had been deflected by defensive end Dexter Manley and returned the ball 10 yards for a touchdown to help the Redskins get to Super Bowl XVII, where they beat the Miami Dolphins.

"All I did was block everything out and just tried to focus. So I didn't get caught up in a lot of the hoopla. I played it pretty close to the vest," said Grant. "I was playing against two of the best in the game at the time [in Dolphins center Dwight Stephenson and guard Bob Kuechenberg]. And they put in the media that they were going to put an iso-cam on Stephenson because he was such a great center.

"I remember getting the article and taking it over to [linebacker] Neal Olkewicz and saying, 'For the first time in Super Bowl history, they're going to have an iso-cam on the center. There is no way they're going to be running plays backward and forward of him pasting us to the ground! We're going to make sure when they turn that camera on and start watching, it's going to be us whooping him!'"

Washington returned the following year for Super Bowl XVIII against the Raiders. And while the iso-cam was focused elsewhere, it appeared that, given the loss, so were the Redskins.

"I think definitely they were better that day. That goes without saying. I think we got stung with a little bit of believing what we were hearing, as far as we'll be the greatest team ever or this is a dynasty," Grant said. "I've been on both sides of that coin and I know what happened to the Raiders. [They] had to sit back and listen to all the media about how great we were. They were sitting there taking it all in.

"The same thing happened to us with Miami [in Super Bowl XVII], going against [head coach] Don Shula, the legend. They got all the attention, and we had to sit back and eat all of that until the game came to prove to the world that we were a team to be reckoned with.

"The same thing happened when we played Denver [and won in Super Bowl XXII]. Denver was the favorite. We go out to press day, and nobody wanted to talk to us. We had the early shift, and then about noon, all the media came and they were all over [the Broncos]. You sit there and you feed off of that and you can't wait until the game happens. I think that's what happened with the Raiders. They had a good team, no doubt, but they came out and laid it on us. It was a terrible loss. To me, losing the Super Bowl, you feel you'd be better off not even coming. It's the lowest of lows."

Joe Jacoby

After making the Redskins as an undrafted free agent in 1981, Joe Jacoby played football's answer to musical chairs. He started two games at left guard, three games at right tackle, and then finally settled in at left tackle, where he started eight games. His versatility was recognized and rewarded by being named to the Pro Football Writers Association's All-Rookie Team.

The following year, during the strike-shortened 1982 campaign, Jacoby and the rest of the team were recognized after winning Super Bowl XVII over Miami.

"You never think you would be involved," said Jacoby. "First, making a National Football League team and then two years later, playing in the Super Bowl. It went beyond what anybody could've imagined. And then during the years I played, to be involved with it more than once, it's hard to put into words. I guess looking back on it now, you're the last game of the year besides the Pro Bowl and you've got over 100 million people watching you [on television]. So when you think about that, that's pretty neat."

Something that was even better than pretty neat for the Redskins and their fans was that over the next nine years they'd play in three more Super Bowls and be crowned as champions twice. Jacoby feels that the successes were a result of total team efforts.

"I think the key was Coach [Joe] Gibbs and the staff. Staring with not just Coach Gibbs, but [Redskins owner] Mr. [Jack Kent] Cooke, [general managers] Bobby Beathard and Charley Casserly, and the people we had all the way from Mr. Cooke on down. That's everybody working towards one common goal. Everybody had their responsibilities and knew what they were supposed to do. Nobody was looking over their shoulder.

"Coach Gibbs ran the offense and had his responsibilities and he had the assistant coaches doing their jobs. So it was everybody working together, and then you had to put the pieces on the field together with the players."

Tim Johnson

In an attempt to utilize his quickness and size, the Redskins shifted Tim Johnson from defensive end to defensive tackle after acquiring him from Pittsburgh in 1990.

The move paid off the following year when Washington finished the regular season at 14–2, its best mark since having the same record in 1983. What was the key?

"I think Coach Gibbs [has] genius [in] his ability to put players in the right place and to pick the right players," said Johnson. "He went out and got me and [defensive end] Eric Williams and a couple other guys. He began to build that team, and that was the genius of that team. Coach Gibbs knew the right players that were going to fit. He didn't have to go find the most talented high-round draft-choice player, because I wasn't. I was a sixth-round draft choice [in 1987].

"In Pittsburgh, I was in a 3-4 [defensive alignment] playing end. In Washington, I was in a 4-3 playing inside [at tackle]. I call it genius because I was out of position, but evidently, they saw my ability to be able to play inside without seeing me play inside. It was masterful the way they put that team together. Putting the right people on the team and [putting them] in the right position, that's hard to do."

The right people at the right positions were hardly challenged in the playoffs. They flew past the Atlanta Falcons, 24–7, and then destroyed the Detroit Lions, 41–10, for the NFC title. Washington's momentum continued in Super Bowl XXVI when they beat the Buffalo Bills.

"It was like a dream almost," Johnson said. "What's funny is that I was on the sideline [prior to the game], just hyped like everybody else,

and as I was standing there, [my former coach with the Steelers] Chuck
Noll comes up behind me and taps me on my rear. I looked around and
I think, 'Man, the Lord has a sense of humor, doesn't he? A couple of
years ago, I was stuck in Pittsburgh and now look! [Noll's] watching me
play in the Super Bowl.' So that was kind of a funny moment. It was
funny how he acknowledged me. I almost said, 'Thanks for trading me
because it worked out better this way.'"

Billy Kilmer

The Redskins entered the 1971 season with a surprise. Sonny Jurgensen,
who had been expected to be the starting quarterback, was sidelined
during the preseason with an injured shoulder. Billy Kilmer, who had
been acquired in a trade with New Orleans and was not initially too
pleased to be heading north, stepped in and led Washington to its first
playoff berth in 26 years.

That turned out to be just an appetizer because the entrée arrived to
the table in 1972. With Kilmer under center for a majority of the year,
the Redskins posted an 11–3 record and beat their division rival Dallas
Cowboys for the NFC championship.

"That was probably my most memorable season because of the
team's success," said Kilmer, who was in his 10th of 16 seasons in the NFL
with the 49ers, Saints, and Redskins. "Of course, it was one of my better
years that I played. The only bad thing about that year was that we didn't
win the Super Bowl—and we were favored going in, too. We didn't win
it! That was the only disappointing part of it."

Disappointing is as good a word as any to describe Washington's and
Kilmer's performances in Super Bowl VII against Miami. He finished the
game 14-of-28 for 104 yards and threw three interceptions. The
Redskins finished the game on the short side of a 14–7 score and
watched the Dolphins cap the NFL's only undefeated season.

"It was the only game I ever played [that started] at 12:00 noon [actu-
ally, 12:30]," Kilmer said of the game that was played in Los Angeles'
Memorial Coliseum. "I don't know why they wanted to play it at 12:00
noon. I guess so it'd be on [television] at 3:00 Eastern Time.

"It wasn't really a well-played game on either team's side. We didn't play real well offensively and of course, I didn't [play well]."

Jim Lachey

It was just a matter of time. Chosen in the first round of the 1985 NFL Draft by San Diego, offensive tackle Jim Lachey was named to the all-rookie teams of UPI, *Football Digest*, and the Pro Football Writers of America.

Two years later, he concluded the season and his tenure with the Chargers by playing for the AFC squad in the Pro Bowl. And in 1990, his third season in Washington after a trade with the Raiders, with whom he played just one game in 1988, the remarkable left tackle was the top vote-getter at tackle for the Pro Bowl and was honored as the NFC's Offensive Lineman of the Year.

"I think it all came together in 1990, '91," said Lachey. "I really learned the difference at that time in the AFC and NFC. The AFC, obviously, was a little bit more of a passing and speed conference, where the NFC, especially the NFC East, is more of a power conference. I need to, as an offensive lineman, change my game and adapt to what Coach Gibbs and [offensive line] Coach [Joe] Bugel wanted me to do. I think once I learned exactly what they wanted me to do, we started having some fun."

Winning certainly enhanced the fun that the Redskins were enjoying. In 1990 they were 10–6 and advanced to the playoffs as a wild-card team. But after beating Philadelphia, they were sent home by San Francisco. The following year, with a 14–2 record, tops in the NFL, Washington was the team waving good-bye to its opponents. The final time was to the Buffalo Bills in Super Bowl XXVI.

"Sometimes you think when you're struggling, especially on the Chargers, about not making the playoffs," Lachey said. "And then when we missed it with the Redskins the first year I was there, you're thinking, 'Oh, oh. What's happening here? Am I going to get a shot at it?'

"Guys talk about it. I played with Dan Fouts, Charlie Joiner, Ed White, and Donny Macek, guys like that with the Chargers who played a lot of years and never had a Super Bowl ring. So I know how important it was and I appreciated it. I had appreciation for the game the way Coach Gibbs and the organization did it."

Chip Lohmiller

By 1991, his fourth season in the NFL, Chip Lohmiller had shown why the Redskins had used their top draft choice in 1988 on the place-kicker. He was in the league's record book for booting a field goal in 28 consecutive games, and in 1991, had led the NFC in scoring with 149 points.

"The offense moved the ball so well that they gave me a lot of opportunities to kick those field goals," said Lohmiller. "So it wasn't all me. It was basically that our offensive package was so strong that it put me in a position to score a lot of points."

Those points came in handy during Washington's journey to the Super Bowl XXVI victory over Buffalo. What made the game even more special for Lohmiller was that it was played in his hometown of Minneapolis, Minnesota.

"I had to come up with 77 tickets! That was a big bill for me, and all of my buddies never paid me back," laughed Lohmiller. "But it was very nice to go back and play in front of the fans that I had [while] playing at the University of Minnesota and in high school.

"That was a tremendous year. We had a great group of guys that played so well together, it was just like a family. Off the field, we did things together. On the field, we jelled as a team. We clicked. Everybody got along and we'd just do what it takes to win."

Charles Mann

It is understandable that rookie defensive end Charles Mann was a little naïve about what would take place after the Redskins rolled through the 1983 season with a 14–2 record and met the Raiders in Super Bowl XVIII. It was, after all, only the 19th NFL game he had played in.

"It was way more than I could have ever expected," Mann said. "I had no idea what a Super Bowl was like, and leading up to it, and the hoopla, and the way we won that season. [Looking back,] that was probably the best team I'd ever been on. Yet, we didn't finish it and win the Super Bowl."

The results were different four seasons later when Washington returned to meet Denver in Super Bowl XXII. And even though Mann had been through the championship experience before, it wasn't any less challenging.

"I don't think any Super Bowl run is easy," said Mann. "You've got to stay focused. You're a couple of plays away from not making it, so every play counts. Every play is important. It was tough. Just like all of them were."

Mann played for a third Lombardi Trophy and helped the Redskins earn another championship four years later when they beat Buffalo in Super Bowl XXVI.

Martin Mayhew

In 1991, his second full season as the starting cornerback opposite Darrell Green, Martin Mayhew hauled in three interceptions, one of which he returned for a touchdown, and helped the Redskins post a 14–2 record, sail through the playoffs, and earn a berth in Super Bowl XXVI.

"That was just a great year. A lot of things went right for us," said Mayhew. "We had a solid mix of young players and veteran players. And we stayed pretty much injury-free that year. We had a lot of guys that had career years that year. [Linebacker] Wilber Marshall had a great season. [Defensive end] Charles Mann had a great season.

"And we had some breaks where things went our way. We had games where you had some star players who weren't able to play for whatever reason. We went up against the Lions, and [star running back] Barry Sanders gets hurt in pregame warm-ups and can't play, and we beat them 45–0. So things just kind of fell into place for us. I think Coach Gibbs and [defensive coordinator] Richie Petitbon did a great job using the players that we had and figuring out what those players would be good at and putting us in position to be successful."

Successful is one word to describe Washington's performance against Buffalo on Super Bowl Sunday. *Vengeful* is another word that Mayhew could have used. The Bills had left him unprotected in Plan B free agency after spending the 1988 season on their injured-reserve list.

"Yeah, they were the team that put me on Plan B, which meant that they didn't think that I was going to be a key part of what they were trying to do. So it was satisfying to go up against them and win. It was a lot of fun and a great experience."

Rich Milot

With a 10–6 record in 1979 and a 6–10 mark the following year, linebacker Rich Milot's first two seasons with Washington were a wash. However, the Redskins started anew in 1981 when they replaced Jack Pardee as the head coach with Joe Gibbs.

"Jack Pardee knew the system, but I think that when Joe Gibbs came in, he had a better coaching staff," said Milot. "They were better teachers. [Defensive coordinator] Larry Peccatiello in particular was a better teacher. Jack, I think, assumed you knew a lot. Maybe more than you actually did. I think Larry really helped me with learning the game."

In 1982 Milot and his teammates would have to depend on Gibbs and his assistants to learn how to play in the big game. They concluded that campaign by beating Miami in Super Bowl XVII. The linebacker felt it was an incredible experience.

"That was that much and more, quite honestly. I mean, it was just an exciting time," Milot said. "To be able to go out to California and do it was doubly exciting because I'd really never spent that much time in California. That was just a good time. Everybody was playing together throughout the whole season. That just topped it off."

The Redskins rose to the top again in 1983 but were upset by the AFC champion Raiders in Super Bowl XVIII.

"That was devastating because I think firmly that we had a better team that year. And I wouldn't be surprised if we had the best Redskins team that year that's ever been put on a field. To go there and really actually not even show up....

"I always get the feeling they were spying on us because they knew too many things that we did. They just knew too many things! The flip side, I think they were a looser team. That's the way we were initially when we played Miami in the first Super Bowl. But the second Super Bowl, we just seemed tight. I think that really plays a lot into those types of games."

Milot's nine-year career with the Redskins came to a close in Super Bowl XXII, when Washington, behind Doug Williams' four touchdown passes, erupted for a 35-point second quarter and blew out the Denver Broncos.

"You've got to be surprised at a second quarter like that," said Milot. "I thought we matched up really well against them, but nobody could have expected that to happen. It seems like if it was a chess match, Denver made all the wrong moves that day. They were slanting to the wrong side just about every play that we had a play going in the other direction."

The Redskins seemed to be going in the right direction during much of Milot's tenure with the team, evidenced by the three NFC titles and two Super Bowl championships. He feels that Washington's success started with its owner, Jack Kent Cooke.

"You have to go to the very top," Milot said. "We had an owner that was demanding and he was smart enough to hire Joe Gibbs. And again, I go back to his staff. I think he had a great staff of teachers. In football, that's where you've got to start. You have to have a good coaching staff. But ultimately, when you start winning, you get a camaraderie together, and I think it's easier to keep winning that way."

Brian Mitchell

Brian Mitchell did not have to toil too long in the NFL before he had an opportunity to suit up on Super Bowl Sunday. In 1991, just his second season, the kickoff and punt returner helped Washington reach Super Bowl XXVI against Buffalo.

Was he nervous to be playing on football's biggest stage? That would be a no.

"I was so excited and young that I didn't have a chance to be nervous, to be honest with you," said Mitchell, who had one kickoff return for 16 yards. "You know, people say when you're young, you're just dumb enough to not even know. I think that was the situation.

I don't know if it was nervousness because I wasn't really, like, shaking or had any butterflies [in my stomach], but it was such an exciting moment, being a young kid looking at the Super Bowl, that by the time I realized we were playing in the Super Bowl, it was the second quarter. The first quarter was gone."

The Redskins were, well, pretty ticked off when they took the field, to say the least. The offense came through with 417 total yards, while the defensive unit intercepted Bills quarterback Jim Kelly four times and sacked him on five occasions. They also held Buffalo's star running back, Thurman Thomas, to just 13 yards on 10 carries.

"Well, I thought we were a better team," Mitchell said. "Then again, they did a lot of talking during the week, which motivated us a lot more. The week of practice was probably the most intense week of practice I've ever seen on that team. And I'm talking about even training camp. We got so fired up about [what] they were calling our [offensive] linemen; they said they were fat. 'The Hogs, yeah, they're fat, they're sloppy.'

"[And] they were arguing back and forth with each other about who was going to be the MVP of the Super Bowl as if we weren't there! We took that seriously and went out there and showed them we were way more physical than they were. They were a bunch of guys in the AFC, and that was a pass-happy league at that time. And we just took the physical to them, and they couldn't handle it."

John Riggins

Eleventh-year running back John Riggins had one request as the Redskins went into in the strike-induced four-round NFL playoffs that capped off the 1982 campaign. He wanted the ball more. Second-year head coach Joe Gibbs obliged.

After gaining 119 yards in the first-round victory over Detroit, Riggins ran the ball 37 times for a career-high 185 yards in the second-round win against Minnesota. And in the NFC Championship Game, Riggins carried the ball 36 times for 140 yards to help Washington top its division rival Dallas Cowboys.

And then, relying on the credo "if it ain't broke, don't fix it," the Redskins attached their desire to earn their first Lombardi Trophy on

Coach Joe Gibbs (right) and Super Bowl MVP John Riggins (center) congratulate Redskins owner Jack Kent Cooke following their victory in Super Bowl XVII.

Riggins' rushing abilities against Miami and its AFC-best defense, in Super Bowl XVII.

The decision to pin their hopes on Riggins was tested when, with a little more than 10 minutes left in the fourth quarter and trailing the Dolphins 17–13, Washington faced fourth-and-1 from Miami's 43-yard line. The Redskins decided to go for a first down.

"It was an interesting moment," said Riggins. "There were probably 100,000 people [in the Rose Bowl] for the game, and they knew. The countless millions [watching on television], they knew what we were going to do."

It's likely that the Dolphins did as well, but it wouldn't matter. Riggins took the handoff from Redskins quarterback Joe Theismann and started to run around the left end. Miami cornerback Don McNeal met him for a brief moment at the 40 before he was on the ground and could only watch as Riggins raced the rest of the way down the sideline for the score, then the longest touchdown run from scrimmage in Super Bowl history. That gave Washington its first lead of the game, 20–17.

"Theismann handed the ball off and he had the best seat in the house," Riggins said. "It was one of those plays where everything fell into place, and the fact that Don McNeal had slipped a little bit, that kept him from getting a clean shot at me. He might have slowed me down more. I was only thinking about the first down. I wasn't thinking about the touchdown. That just came along. Of course, it was 43 yards away, so I'm waiting for someone to hit me, and that never happened."

Following Washington's next possession, the Dolphins never had a chance. Riggins carried the ball eight times during the 12-play drive that took nearly seven minutes off the clock and ended with a six-yard touchdown pass from Theismann to Charlie Brown. The Redskins won their first championship in 40 years, 27–17.

Riggins, who wanted to carry the ball more during the playoffs, carried off the MVP award after setting Super Bowl records with 38 carries for 166 yards.

"Because I was the MVP and a slow dresser, I was by far the last person out of the locker room. Everyone was gone. It's just vacant, no one there," said Riggins. "I walked out onto the playing field and I remember looking up. It's getting dusky; it's going into the gloaming. You see the workers up in the stands sweeping the cups up. They left the scoreboard on, and I remember seeing the score: Redskins 27, Dolphins 17. It was that moment of truth where I'm like, 'Damn, I'm a world champion.'"

Mark Rypien

By rattling off 11 straight victories to open the 1991 season, the Redskins were clearly en route to a conference title and a date with Buffalo in Super Bowl XXVI.

Quarterback Mark Rypien, who was named as the NFC Player of the Year, feels that the reason the team enjoyed so much success started with the bespectacled man wearing a headset on the sideline.

"It was Joe Gibbs' ability to keep veteran players around, his system, and selling his players on the system," said Rypien. "I think that [enables] you to be successful."

Mark Rypien threw for 292 yards in the Redskins' 37–24 victory over the Buffalo Bills in Super Bowl XXVI.

Gibbs' system brought about continued success on Super Bowl Sunday and earned his team a third Lombardi Trophy. During the game, which was not as close as the final score would indicate, the Redskins totaled 417 yards of total offense compared to Buffalo's 283. For his part, Rypien completed 18-of-33 passes for 292 yards with two touchdowns and was named as the game's Most Valuable Player.

And although he was clearly delighted about the outcome, Rypien didn't feel the experience as a whole was what he expected. "I think the Super Bowls are not for the teams that are involved, it's more for corporate America to have a big gathering at a football game," said Rypien. "Your fan base is not nearly the same as you would have at RFK Stadium. You get some people that are fanatic about it no matter what that was able to get there, but it's a different fan base.

"Joe Gibbs was so good about giving us some leeway when we had a chance on Monday and Tuesday. And then we had to buckle down on Wednesday, Thursday, Friday, and Saturday, and up to the game and just understand that we're here to finish off something very special. So from that standpoint, I don't think anything really changed. We were in a different city and practicing in a different facility, but other than that, it was business as usual.

"The game was somewhat different because there is so much put into that thing, so much drama to the whole thing that it didn't really feel like a playoff game or NFC Championship Game or something in your own stadium and in front of your own people."

Ricky Sanders

Ricky Sanders was destined to be in a burgundy-and-gold spotlight.

Following two seasons with Houston in the USFL, the Redskins acquired the receiver in a trade with New England less than a month before the 1986 season got underway. Then after being shelved for the first five games because of leg injuries, Sanders' first reception in the NFL was a 71-yarder from Jay Schroeder against the Giants on October 27. Two weeks later, on November 9, he and Schroeder hooked up on a 26-yard toss in Green Bay for the receiver's first touchdown.

Evidenced by what occurred during the 1987 postseason, he was just getting warmed up. After helping Washington advance to Super Bowl XXII against Denver, Sander's fingerprints would be left all over the league championship game's all-time record book.

As a team, the Redskins set one mark by scoring 35 points on five touchdowns during the second quarter. Sanders crossed the goal line with the ball for two of those scores.

The first: trailing 10–0, Washington had Doug Williams in at quarterback. And on first down from his own 20-yard line, he lobbed the ball to the right sideline that Sanders, who was on a fly pattern, grabbed and raced 80 yards with for a touchdown.

The second: after fellow receiver Gary Clark caught a 27-yard touchdown pass and running back Timmy Smith raced 58 yards for another score, Williams and Sanders teamed up again for a 50-yard touchdown pass play.

Sanders helped secure the Lombardi Trophy with a nine-catch performance for a then–Super Bowl record 193 yards and two touchdowns.

"It was a natural high that you can't compare. It was exciting. It was a good day," said Sanders. "Doug and I had a great combination. We were on the practice team together [in 1986], and so he threw the ball to me almost every day, 10 to 15 times. So when he got into the starting position and I got into the starting position, it was just like practice."

Sanders had one more catch that did not appear in the statistics. However, just like the ones he caught in the Super Bowl, it received widespread recognition.

With scores of cameras rolling during a ceremony on the White House lawn, President Ronald Reagan stepped up to the podium on the stage, flanked by Redskins players and coaches, and with a football in his hand asked, 'Where's Ricky Sanders?'

"'Where's Ricky Sanders?' Have I done something wrong? I didn't do it! No, not this time," chuckled Sanders, who, while dressed in a suit and tie, ran a crossing pattern in front of the secret service agents. "He had a good arm! He threw a nice, tight spiral. And, yeah, he had a chance [to make it] in the NFL."

Joe Theismann

Having experienced only two postseason games—one as a rookie playing on special teams in 1974, and one as a backup quarterback two years later—Joe Theismann and the Redskins were due.

And in 1982, his fifth season as a full-time starter, and Joe Gibbs' second season as the head coach, they collected. Washington whipped through the strike-interrupted season while Theismann did the same to opposing defenses. The highest-rated quarterback in the NFC, he completed 63.9 percent of his passes and moved the Redskins through three playoff games before meeting and beating Miami in Super Bowl XVII, 27–17.

"It's unreal. It's really beyond description when you win it. I'm sure there are guys that say it's another game and that's okay, terrific, wonderful. But I always played with a lot of emotion. I live my life with a lot of emotion, and it was a very emotional time for us. Winning your first Super Bowl is better than anything. It's better than your first kiss. It's better than your first you know what. That's just the way I look at it. It was better than my first marriage," laughed Theismann.

With the way that things turned out the following year in Super Bowl XVIII, maybe the first Mrs. Theismann was a Raiders fan. The Silver and Black walloped Washington by 29 points, 38–9. Did the Redskins go into the game overconfident that they'd be bringing home another Lombardi Trophy?

"No, there are a couple of things," Theismann said. "First of all, [by totaling just 90 yards on 32 carries] we weren't really able to run the football very effectively. And they made a lot of big plays. [Cornerback] Jeris White almost had Marcus [Allen] on that big [74-yard touchdown] run of his. He almost got him for a six-yard loss. We get a punt blocked. I throw an interception. They run a punt back. They hit big plays. They get a big run. They came up with a lot of big plays, and we couldn't come up with anything.

"And I played bad. MVP of the league, you feel like you're a really good team, you're picked to win, and all of a sudden you go out and you don't play well. That's disheartening. I wasn't overconfident, I just didn't focus."

Rick "Doc" Walker

Washington's veteran tight end and Santa Ana, California, native Rick "Doc" Walker experienced a homecoming when he went to wrap up the 1982 season by playing for the Lombardi Trophy. The Redskins had won the NFC title and were meeting Miami in Super Bowl XVII at the Rose Bowl in Pasadena, California.

"It was home for me. That was a dream come true, to have the biggest game in the universe in your backyard. That was pretty interesting, 62 tickets [for family and friends] later. That was quite an experience," laughed Walker. "The hotel [that the team was staying at] was two miles from my mother's house, and we were able to feed most of the team at my mom's. She fed 50 guys, easily. I don't know anybody that didn't make it over. It was a zoo! We had a chance to get out of the hotel environment. It really kind of broke the ice.

"It was a quick, quick week. And it was highly exciting. You were totally exhausted from all the entertainment demands, practice, and family. It's overwhelming. And it was following the biggest win, I think, in franchise history. That was the biggest problem; being able to garner that type of enthusiasm and intensity two weeks in a row. For all practical purposes, our game [at home against Dallas for the NFC championship on January 22] was bigger than the Super Bowl because it was [played in front of] all our people, our fans. It was really the most amazing environment I'd ever witnessed."

That proved to be an eventful season all the way around—from the dog days of training camp when the offensive linemen and tight ends were given the nickname "Hogs" by assistant coach Joe Bugel, to when those same players led the way for John Riggins to run over the Dolphins, 27–17, on Super Sunday.

"It helps the team to have its identity stamped on its forehead," Walker said. "In Pittsburgh, it was the Steel Curtain. When Dallas was really good, it had Doomsday; the Minnesota Vikings with the Purple People Eaters; and the Raiders were the Raiders.

"I think it helped the players. If you're an offensive player, the Hogs had an impact on everybody. Our receivers blocked as well as, if not better than, any receiver group in the league. A lot of the success of

Riggo's and Joe [Washington's] runs were because guys were downfield chipping people constantly. Not just on certain plays. I just think it was infectious. It made everybody want to get in and get dirty. I just think those things mattered, and I think it's easier for the coaches because you don't have to go around and say everything. The guys understood it and they policed themselves."

Don Warren

When the Redskins took the field to play in Super Bowls XVII, XVIII, XXII, and XXVI, they had the same player line up as the starting tight end—Don Warren.

"The Super Bowl that really stands out to me, that I remember the most, is the very first one because we were all young and we had a young [offensive] line going against the 'Killer Bees,'" said Warren, who had five receptions for 28 yards against the Miami Dolphins.

"[Jeff] Bostic and I were in the hotel the night before, and I was listening to somebody like Jimmy the Greek on TV, and he basically said that we were going to get killed. Bostic and I just kind of looked at each other and said, 'We'll see.' Obviously the game ended in our favor [with a 27–17 victory], and everything turned out good. But I think that's the one that really meant a lot to me because everybody didn't give us a chance."

Doug Williams

After making two starts and earning a couple of key saves during the 1987 season, if Doug Williams had been a baseball pitcher, he would have contended for the Cy Young Award. Fortunately for the Redskins, he was a quarterback. And even more fortunate for them, he was under center in Super Bowl XXII against Denver.

But it was not going to be easy. Late in the first quarter and trailing 10–0, Williams suffered a hyperextended knee and was forced to the sideline to be examined and treated by the team's medical staff. "The only thing that was going through my mind was I was hoping I wasn't hurt bad enough to leave the football game," Williams said. "That was

Quarterback Doug Williams led the Redskins to victory in Super Bowl XXII and also took home the game's MVP award. Photo courtesy of Getty Images

the number-one priority. I hyperextended it, and it was bad. I got some treatment. You do what you have to do."

The treatment that Williams received did the trick, and he returned to the game with 14:17 left in the first half. Shortly after that, bum knee and all, he and his teammates began to make Super Bowl history.

Fifty-three seconds into the second quarter, and with a first down from his own 20-yard line, Williams put the ball up against the right sideline. Ricky Sanders snared the pass and raced 80 yards for Washington's first touchdown.

"That pass basically was supposed to be a seven-yard hitch. The defense dictated what we did on that play," said Williams. "It wasn't a called 80-yarder. It was a called hitch pass just to try to get things rolling. The defensive back played it a different way. He came up to press and jam and he missed the jam. Ricky got by him and it was easy."

At the 4:45 mark with the score 10–7, Williams put the Redskins ahead with a 27-yard scoring pass to Gary Clark.

"Actually, Gary shouldn't have been the receiver. When we sat there and watched it, the ball should have went in the flat to the back, Kelvin Bryant. It was a 'hot' situation, which means they had a blitz on, but the linebacker didn't get there. Even if he'd got there, he wouldn't have got there in time to stop me from throwing the football. Gary was wide open."

Following halfback Timmy Smith's 58-yard touchdown run to put Washington up 21–10, Williams and Sanders connected along the right sideline again. This time, Sanders found the end zone from 50 yards away.

"Remember, we were running the counter, and they had to respect Timmy Smith," Williams said. "And basically, it was just a play-action off the counter. The free safety came up to make the play, and Ricky got behind him, and it was a cake-walk."

Washington's record-breaking fifth touchdown of the quarter came after cornerback Barry Wilburn intercepted Broncos quarterback John Elway, giving the Redskins the ball at their own 21-yard line. Williams then engineered a 79-yard drive that was capped off when he spotted tight end Clint Didier in the back corner of the end zone from eight yards out with 1:04 left on the clock before halftime. Washington went into the break with a 25-point lead.

"Clint ran a corner route, and with Gary and Ricky on the ends, you've got to be more concerned with those guys than you are with Clint Didier. He just slipped out there," Williams said.

The Redskins set a record with 35 points in a quarter and held Denver scoreless in the second half, winning 42–10. Williams, who completed 18-of-29 passes for 340 yards and four touchdowns, was named as the game's MVP.

"That wasn't big. You know why? Because there were so many other people out there who were MVPs," said Williams. "Let's talk about 204 yards [rushing] by Timmy Smith. Ricky Sanders had 193 yards in receptions. The offensive line blocked their asses off. And I think Barry Wilburn had what, two interceptions? So there could have been a number of people been MVP in that game, I just happened to be one of them.

"When we went out there, we didn't have any doubt that we were going to win that football game. Maybe the people in Vegas and most of America who were caught up in [my being the first] black quarterback [to start in a Super Bowl] did. But we went out there and had the best week of practice we ever had in our life. We knew what we were going to do! I mean, man for man, pound for pound, we had the best football team."

chapter 4

"Slingin' Sammy"

A Star from the Start

In a move that would come back to haunt them for years, when the still wet-behind-the-ears NFL held its draft on December 12, 1936, more than half of the teams in the league—Brooklyn, Philadelphia, Pittsburgh, the Chicago Cardinals, and the New York Giants—passed over Texas Christian University's two-time All-American Sammy Baugh while making their first-round selections.

The Redskins selected the quarterback with the sixth pick. However, truth be told, he could not have cared any less. "I didn't know a thing about pro football when I got out of TCU," said Baugh. "I didn't know how many teams they had and didn't care too damn much about it. Just those east of the Mississippi River did, really."

Had Baugh crossed the river and traveled to Washington before? "Oh, hell no!" With that little tidbit settled, when he did arrive, it was about the same time as the Redskins were unpacking after their move from Boston.

And as legend has it, during the early days of the team's training camp to prepare for the 1937 season, Redskins head coach Ray Flaherty told the rookie quarterback that even though passes were not a common offensive game plan in the league, his throwing attempts would have to be accurate. Flaherty suggested that he aim the football toward the receiver's eyes. To which Baugh simply replied, "Which eye?"

Was it a sign of cockiness? Perhaps. But if he could back it up, it more likely demonstrated confidence. Baugh could back it up. And,

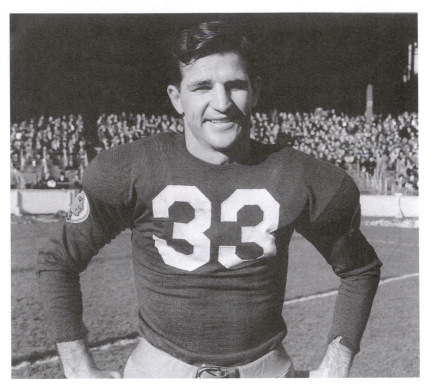

"Slingin'" Sammy Baugh was a charter member of the Pro Football Hall of Fame in 1963.

quite frankly, he soon showed that he could pass the football unlike anyone else the league had ever witnessed.

During his first season, Baugh led the league by completing 81 of 171 passes for 1,127 yards—over 300 yards more than second-leading passer Pat Coffee of Chicago—and eight touchdowns. Washington outscored its opponents 195–120 and finished the season with an 8–3 record.

"I thought my first year up there we had a real good ballclub. We played both ways, so we had a good defensive ballclub and a good offensive ballclub, and that's about all you can ask," Baugh said. "We had a good bunch of boys. We had an All-Pro tackle [Turk Edwards], we had an All-Pro end [Wayne Millner], and we had an All-Pro running back [Cliff Battles]."

After winning the Eastern Division, the Redskins went on to meet the Bears at Chicago's Wrigley Field on December 12 in the NFL Championship Game. Washington won, 28–21. However, Baugh remembers more about the title game than what was on the scoreboard.

"It was the worst field I ever played on," said Baugh, who completed 18 of 33 passes for 335 yards and three touchdowns in 15-degree weather. "An icy field, you couldn't get very good footage. You were sliding all the time. It was as cold a day as I can ever remember. It was a bad day."

Baugh Owned the '40s

Redskins quarterback Sammy Baugh approached the decade of the 1940s just as he did as a rookie in 1937—by scattering passes all over the field in a fashion that had been unseen before in the NFL. That season, he led the league with 1,127 passing yards, was named All-Pro, and guided Washington to the league's championship game, where they beat the Chicago Bears, 28–21.

In 1940, behind Baugh, the Redskins began using the T formation on offense and opened the season with a seven-game winning streak. They closed the campaign with a 9–2 record and were back in the NFL Championship Game on December 8 against the Bears. Only this time Chicago captured its revenge and ripped the Redskins, 73–0.

In a 1999 Associated Press article, Baugh said that there was something more behind the lopsided score than Washington's failures to find its own end zone or to keep the Bears out of theirs. He believed that some of his teammates were infuriated with Redskins owner George Preston Marshall and, because of that, did not play up to their potential.

"[Marshall] put things in the paper running the Bears down," said Baugh. "You don't want to help the other team. You shouldn't say things like that. It made us so mad, they decided not to play. Look at the game! How many times do you beat a team in a real close game [7–3] and two [actually, three] weeks later you can't do a thing?

"They turned on Mr. Marshall. They had been running him down for a year. I never talked to the league because I didn't have any proof, and I still don't. It doesn't keep me from thinking, though."

Washington's rivalry with Chicago continued with another show-down in the 1942 championship game. This time the Redskins came out on top, 14–6.

The 1943 season could have been written in bold print and capital letters on the multi-position star's résumé. Not only did Baugh lead the NFL in passing for a third time with 1,754 yards and 23 touchdowns, as a defensive back, he led the league with 11 interceptions and was the top punter for the fourth consecutive year with a 45.9 average.

"I guess that was probably the best year I had as far as that goes," Baugh said. "Hell, you just played. If you're a football player, you go play football. You don't give a damn who you're playing, you go do your best every time you get out there. I had a little too much pride to look bad."

Baugh looked anything but bad on November 23, 1947, when the Redskins hosted the Chicago Cardinals on appropriately enough "Sammy Baugh Day." Washington had lost its last five games and was on its way to a dismal 4–8 record. The Cardinals, meanwhile, came into the game winning seven of their eight games en route to a 9–3 mark and the NFL championship.

But that afternoon, the only record that football fans would be talking about belonged to Baugh. He was, in a word, *incredible*. With 355 yards and six touchdown passes, he led the Redskins to a 45–21 upset victory.

"[Prior to the game] they were already on the field, all those [offensive] linemen, [and] they told me, 'You're not even going to get your uniform dirty today.' And it was already a little muddy out there," said Baugh. "They said, 'We're going to beat them!' And by God, we didn't have that good a ballclub that year and we beat them. That was the biggest surprise that I had back then because that team played a great ballgame."

Baugh, enshrined as a charter member of the Pro Football Hall of Fame in 1963, wrapped up his 16-year Redskins career following the 1952 season with 21,866 passing yards and 187 touchdowns, a team record he still holds. He also picked off 31 passes and averaged 45.1 yards on 338 punts.

chapter 5

Washington's Field Generals

Battered, Bruised, and Only One Win

It's not often when a player can suit up for the NFL team that he followed as a kid, but Norm Snead had just that opportunity after Washington made him its first-round draft choice in 1961. And having been raised in Newport News, Virginia, the quarterback was well aware of what he was getting into. Specifically, that the Redskins had had only three winning seasons over the previous 15 years, most recently in 1955 when they were 8–4 under head coach Joe Kuharich.

When Snead reported to the team, he found a new home, D.C. Stadium; a new coach, Bill McPeak; and a vacant locker that had been used the prior season by then-starting quarterback, Ralph Guglielmi, who had moved on to the St. Louis Cardinals. However, not having a veteran sounding board didn't concern Snead or disrupt his confidence.

"I knew I could be an NFL quarterback when I first went to training camp," said Snead. "The circumstance of Bill McPeak and [team owner] George Preston Marshall deciding to go with a rookie [as the starting quarterback], I had no control over that. They made the decision based on what they saw.

"I was glad to play. It would have been better if I had a veteran [to show me the ropes], yes, but if it had been a veteran like a young [Dan] Marino or a young anybody, I would have never played. [I would have been his backup.] So I'm glad it turned out that way."

That may have been true, but the season opener on September 17 in San Francisco did not turn out as he would have hoped. The 49ers topped Washington, 35–3. What does Snead remember about his debut?

"That I didn't know what the hell was going on," he laughed. "It just looked like a Chinese fire drill out there. I was excited, I was inexperienced. I was all of those things, and it just looked like mass confusion when you looked at the defense."

The confusion did not really clear up. The Redskins fell short on the scoreboard the next eight games en route to a 1–12–1 record, their second consecutive one-win campaign. "We were a team that basically was building and we just did what we had to do," Snead said. "We would like to have been just like any team. At that time, Green Bay had a great running game and a great passing game, and that's what everybody strives for. We just didn't have that. We started seven rookies. You're not going to win a lot in the NFL starting seven rookies.

"Losing is not fun. We had a bunch of veterans that had to put up with a lot of rookies, and I felt sorry for them. We sort of let them down. But it was a mixed bag of emotions. You had to prove yourself, first of all, to your peers, the people you're playing with. And that was the hardest part. We were competitive in most of the games, but a lot of them we were just very, very poor in. But my biggest concern was my teammates. I didn't want to let them down."

One thing that could be said of Snead's rookie season was that he kept getting back up. Sacks were not a well-kept statistic at that time; however, he experienced quite a few of them.

"I didn't run for my life because I couldn't run. I just got the hell beat out of me," joked Snead, who completed 172 of 375 passes for 2,337 yards with 11 touchdowns and 22 interceptions during that first year. "That's the fault of me as well as the offensive line. That's inexperience; knowing when to get rid of the ball, give yourself some outlets in the rotation of priority receivers, and so forth. You had to know where to go to if one or two or three are covered. And I wasn't very good at that in that first year."

And while beating Dallas at home, 34–24, in the finale on December 17 behind running back Dick James' four touchdowns was one of the few highlights Snead enjoyed that season, another one occurred earlier in the year when he met Redskins' legendary quarterback Sammy Baugh.

"That was an exciting day for me," Snead recalled. "He came to one of our practices, and after practice, he put his arm around me and somebody snapped a picture. I have that picture to this day. The things he told me stuck with me my entire career. He said, 'Forget what people say. You do what you do and let everything take care of itself.'"

Sonny's "Little Added Incentive"

From 1957 to 1963, Sonny Jurgensen would travel to Washington once a year as a member of the division-rival Eagles. The final five trips back to Philadelphia were with a victory.

Those trips, however, became reversed for the veteran quarterback after the Eagles hired Washington's former head coach, Joe Kuharich, in 1964. That's when the last thing Jurgensen thought would occur actually did. He was traded to Washington for fellow quarterback Norm Snead.

"I didn't know why [I was traded] because Joe Kuharich came there, and we had a nice meeting for a couple hours talking about what we were going to do," said Jurgensen, who had been Philadelphia's starter the previous three seasons and owned the team record with 32 touchdown passes in 1961. "I think it was in '63, I had seven ends that broke arms, so I had no receivers to throw to. We'd won [the NFL championship] in '60 and had gone downhill. In '61 we had a good year, but in '62 and '63 we had all kinds of problems. And the problems were physical problems. So the team got old, and we slipped.

"I thought that [Kuharich and I] had a very good meeting, and I went to lunch two or three blocks from the Eagles' office, and somebody came in and said, 'Hey! I see they just traded you to Washington.' I said, 'Aw, don't tell me that. I just left the coach an hour ago.' And he said, 'No, I'm not kidding you, Sonny. They just traded you to the Washington Redskins for Norm Snead.' I said, 'Yeah, I know you're kidding. It's April Fools Day.' And it was. I didn't believe him. And it was true!"

It is also true that the Jurgensen-led Redskins didn't enjoy too many sunny days as the 1964 season got underway. They lost their first four games, albeit three were by less than a touchdown. But when they hosted the 2–2 Eagles on October 11, Jurgensen played as if Washington hadn't lost a game. He threw five touchdown passes as the Redskins popped Philadelphia, 35–20.

"I had given everything I could do, and I think they saw fit to trade us. But I know when I went back to play against them it made a little added incentive," Jurgensen said. "It was a good thing in the long run, but when it happens to you, you're shocked."

The Redskins earned a 21–10 victory when the teams met again on November 1 in Philadelphia. It was the first time they had swept the series since 1958.

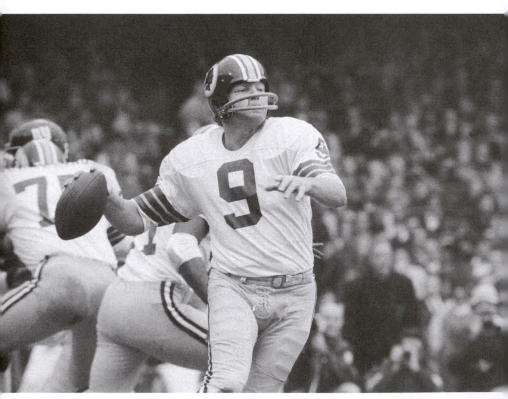

Quarterback Sonny Jurgensen retired at the age of 40 in 1974 after amassing 32,224 career passing yards.

Peaks, Valleys, and Crutches

As one would surely expect, Sonny Jurgensen experienced the gamut of what professional football had to offer during his 11 seasons quarterbacking the Redskins.

In 1966, his third season in Washington after seven with Philadelphia, with Otto Graham, a newly enshrined Hall of Fame quarterback himself, as the new head coach, Jurgensen moved atop of the team's record book. He completed 254 passes, eclipsing Sammy Baugh's mark of 210 set in 1947; he led the NFL with 3,209 passing yards, breaking Norm Snead's 1963 team record by 166 yards; and he connected on 28 touchdown passes, three more than Baugh had posted in 1947.

The Redskins and the NFL had to print new record books again after the following season because Jurgensen apparently was just warming up. He set all-time season-high league records with 508 attempts, 288 completions, and 3,747 yards. And he broke his year-old team record with 31 touchdown passes.

"We had good receivers, and that was the way that we had to move the football. That was our best method of moving the thing," laughed Jurgensen. "That particular year, things fell into place pretty good for us."

But what was not so good was the confidence that Jurgensen had in Graham's ability to lead from the sideline instead of from the huddle.

"It was all new for him. He had been a great quarterback, a great player, and I didn't know," Jurgensen said. "[Redskins owner] Edward Bennett Williams brought him in to be the coach, and his experience was he had coached the [College] All-Star Game. And I'm not sure he was cut out for that. I know that he liked it, and he did it, and we did well offensively, but I don't know that that was his bailiwick. He ran the offense, but you've got to remember when he was with the Cleveland Browns, he didn't call the plays. Paul Brown did. So it was different for him."

Graham was replaced after the 1968 season. During his three years in Washington, the team was 17–22–3.

However, the Redskins were much improved in 1972 under head coach George Allen. After going 11–3 during the regular season, they won the NFC championship, its first title in 30 years, and met Miami in Super Bowl VII. Jurgensen, who had suffered a season-ending leg injury midway through the campaign, could only watch the Redskins lose to the Dolphins, 14–7.

"To have the opportunity to get to the Super Bowl…. That was the most disappointing thing of my career: to get there and be on crutches and not be able to play," said Jurgensen. "[Miami's head coach] Don Shula walked by me on the field before the game, and he said, 'I know how hard you worked to make this happen and I'm sorry that you'll not be able to play. It'd be a better game if you could play.' I thought that was a classy thing right before the game."

Kilmer Comes to the Rescue

Billy Kilmer did not enjoy much success during his four seasons (1967–1970) with the expansion New Orleans Saints. However, he must have impressed at least one opposing team's head coach.

Less than three weeks after taking over the helm of the Redskins in 1971, George Allen, who had spent the previous four seasons patrolling the sideline for the Los Angeles Rams, traded linebacker Tom Roussel and fourth- and eighth-round draft choices to the Saints for the quarterback. Kilmer was, let's just say, less than pleased about the deal.

"I didn't want to come to the Redskins because I knew I was going to have to play behind Sonny Jurgensen," said Kilmer. "I wanted to go somewhere where I could play because I was going to be 32 years old and I knew I didn't have too many more years left [to play], and there were other teams out there that needed a starting quarterback.

"I happened to be in Miami at the Hialeah Race Track when I found out. I told [Allen], 'I appreciate it, but I wish you'd trade me and give me a chance to play somewhere else.' He said, 'Come up here and talk with me.' So I did [about a week after the trade]. That was the day he made the trade for all the Rams. The 'Ramskins,' we'd call them: Diron Talbert, Jack Pardee, Myron Pottios. He told me, 'We're going to have a big winner here.' So I said, 'Well, I'll stick it out for a year.'"

That proved to be a good move. Jurgensen suffered a shoulder injury during a late preseason game in Miami and missed practically the whole year. And so with Kilmer under center, Washington won its first five

Quarterback Billy Kilmer threw for 20,495 yards and 152 touchdowns during his 16-year NFL career.

games, finished the season with a 9–4–1 record, and made the playoffs for the first time in 26 years.

Things got even better for Kilmer and the Redskins the following season. He co-led the NFL with 19 touchdown passes and guided the team to an 11–3 mark and the NFC championship.

"It was pretty exciting. We kind of jazzed up all the fans there," Kilmer said. "If you look back, it was the beginning of a long era in Redskins winning—going from George Allen through Joe Gibbs. I guess we could say that we started the trend. For 30 years before that, they hadn't won anything, hadn't won many games. We got the fans going. It was great!"

Mr. Popular *A* & Mr. Popular *B*

An old adage around the game of football and particularly around the NFL is that the most popular player on the team in the eyes of the fans is the backup quarterback. That appeared to be valid in Washington during the four years, 1971 to 1974, that Billy Kilmer and Sonny Jurgensen were both members of the Redskins. It got to a point where cars around the area were spotted with "I Like Billy" or "I Like Sonny" bumper stickers.

Two things, though. One, it wasn't certain just who the team's backup was. Head coach George Allen moved them up and down the depth chart like he was in a chess match. And two, Kilmer claims there was no ill will between Jurgensen and himself. They shared the there's-no-*I*-in-*team* philosophy.

"As far as Sonny and I were concerned, we didn't want to rock the boat. We had no problems. We got along good. We drank together, had dinner together, and we're still great friends today," said Kilmer. "The big thing between us was that we wanted to be on a winning side and be a winning team. We hadn't played on many winning teams in our careers and we knew that no matter who was in there, we were going to win games. Whoever was going to play, the other guy tried to help. We knew that neither one of us could probably play a whole season physically.

"I think the biggest problem was George was always cognizant of what the press was talking about and what they were doing. So if I lost a game, they'd start jumping down on me, and he'd replace me with Sonny. And then Sonny would play two or three games every year starting in the middle of the season and then he'd get hurt. Then I'd have to come in and finish up the season. It happened that way most of the time."

A Wheel-less Welcome Wagon

Perhaps George Allen was considering the exchange rate when he looked toward Canada to add a quarterback to the Redskins' roster in 1974. Normally one who would seek out seasoned veterans, Allen traded a first-round draft choice to the Miami Dolphins for the rights to 24-year-old Joe Theismann, who had played the previous three seasons with the Toronto Argonauts of the CFL.

"I never had expected Miami to draft me [out of Notre Dame in 1971], but I wasn't going to go there and play behind Bob [Griese]," said Theismann. "And then I looked around, and from my perspective, [the Redskins'] Sonny [Jurgensen] was in his middle thirties, and Billy [Kilmer] was in the same situation, and I said, 'You know, I could go sit on the bench for a couple years behind those guys and hopefully play.' It wound up being a longer period of time than I had anticipated. I patiently waited two years and then I griped for two years."

Theismann played mostly on special teams during the two gripe-free seasons, leading the Redskins in punt returns in 1974. And while he may not have been grumbling about not seeing much time under center, suffice it to say there weren't any choruses heard coming from the quarterbacks' corner of the locker room of him and the two veterans singing "Kumbaya."

"We had no relationship. I replaced Sam Wyche when I came here, and Sam got along with everybody," Theismann said. "And when I came to town, during my press conference, I basically said, 'I didn't come here to sit. I came here to play.' Well, when you're a hot-shot young rookie, and you're coming to the most veteran union team in football, that's not really the way to endear yourself to people. So I basically pissed off Billy and Sonny.

"And then I wrote a book on quarterbacking, and I had a TV commercial, and that sort of really got to them, I think. What people didn't realize is I don't think Billy and Sonny were really that good of friends when George took over. Everybody felt like, and no question, Sonny was the better thrower, but Billy was the guy who George chose because George wanted to run the football. So there was really a difference between the two of them. And one night at the Dancing Crab, they basically formed a pact and said that it no longer mattered which one of them played as long as—and I was referred to as *him* or *he*—as long as *he* didn't play. Me!

"And so I feel responsible for forging a friendship between Billy and Sonny. If you can't find a common likeness, just find a common enemy. I was the common enemy."

Even after Jurgensen had retired and Theismann became the starter in 1978, his relationship with Kilmer didn't grow any closer. "Billy and I used to sit in offensive meetings, and he completely ignored me. Completely ignored me for like eight weeks," said Theismann. "I learned a great lesson in psychology through that period of time. If you really want to get under somebody's skin, don't yell at them, don't get mad at them, ignore them. And then their mind starts to do crazy things. You start thinking, 'Why doesn't he like me? Why doesn't he talk to me?' You really start playing mind games with yourself.

"But I'll have to tell you something. Sonny Jurgensen, I think, is the greatest pure passer that ever played the game of football. And Billy Kilmer is probably one of the toughest football players I've ever known. It wasn't that I didn't have admiration for those two guys; we just all wanted the same thing. I was the kid that wanted something that those two guys had had. They were both starting quarterbacks in the National Football League. I wanted it, and they wanted to keep it. I see Sonny and Billy today, and we say hi and everything. It's water far under a bridge. But at that time, it was tough."

The "Ringmaster" of the Redskins

Fresh off of his first Super Bowl and his first trip to the Pro Bowl, Joe Theismann was as excited for the 1983 season as a class smart aleck spotting a first-time substitute behind the desk of a no-nonsense teacher.

Leading the Redskins to a 14–2 record, the 10th-year veteran quarterback passed for a career-high 3,714 yards and 29 touchdowns. Washington earned the NFC championship and another trip to the Super Bowl while Theismann earned another trip to the Pro Bowl. Only this time, he traveled to Hawaii to play in the game as the NFL's Most Valuable Player.

"There is one man who is really responsible for what I was as a quarterback. Now, [head coach] Joe Gibbs allowed me to play in a great system with great football players, but [assistant coach] Joe Walton taught me how to play the position," said Theismann. "And if it wasn't for Joe Walton's teachings, I could have never been the quarterback that Joe Gibbs would have wanted to run his football team.

"You know what? Eighty-one was sort of an orientation season for us. In '82 I think the reason we won the world championship that season was because we stayed together during the strike. We worked out a lot together. We spent a lot of time together. And I'm a firm believer that the time you spend on the practice field and the time you spend together in meeting rooms is important, but I don't know if it is as important as the

Joe Theismann led the Redskins to victory in Super Bowl XVII and still holds the team record for most career passing yards.

time you spend together away from those things. You build camaraderie. You build a care and a concern and a respect for the men you play with. That's one thing we had, we were a very close group of guys."

Theismann continued. "We had our own little cliques. There were the Hogs, which was our offensive line. And then we had [receivers who were called] the Smurfs, which was Alvin Garrett, Virgil Seay, and Charlie Brown. Our linebackers were like a SWAT team. They were all dressed in camouflage when we got off the plane [to play in Super Bowl XVII]. [Running back] John Riggins was a circus unto himself. I was not the quarterback of the Washington Redskins; I was this ringmaster of a three-ring circus called the Washington Redskins. It was an entertaining, fun, crazy group of guys. I've always described them as characters with character."

One Play, Two Directions

A *Monday Night Football* television audience and 53,371 fans who were at RFK Stadium on November 18, 1985, witnessed veteran quarterback Joe Theismann's 12-year career come to an end and second-year quarterback Jay Schroeder's career basically begin on the same play.

Looking to improve their record to 6–5, the Redskins hosted the division rival New York Giants, who entered the game with a 7–3 mark and riding a four-game winning streak. But for several moments during the second quarter, not many people really cared about the standings.

While Theismann tried to execute a flea-flicker, three of New York's linebackers, including Lawrence Taylor, converged on him at the same time. The forceful contact resulted with the quarterback on the turf with a broken leg. And after he was carted off the field, Schroeder buckled his chinstrap and confidently commandeered Washington's huddle like a seasoned pro.

"I prepared every week like I was going to play. I think that's the only way you can do it. If you don't, then you're going to be in trouble," said Schroeder. "So I thought I was mentally prepared. I was physically prepared. Whenever the time came, I was going to go in and do what the good Lord blessed me with the ability to do. I was just fortunate that it was that night and things turned out the way they did.

"The first pass that I had a chance to throw, Art Monk lays out and catches a 44-yard pass down the sideline. That, I think, will stick with me for a while. It was kind of fun to watch everybody react and go from there. I mean, you're playing on *Monday Night Football*! You're playing against the Giants, a big-time rival in the NFC East with Lawrence Taylor, Gary Reasons, Harry Carson, and all those guys. You name them, and they were there. And here I am playing in a game after almost five years of not playing any football [because of a four-year baseball stint in the Toronto Blue Jays organization following a college career at UCLA]."

Schroeder tossed 12 other completions and finished 13-of-21 for 221 yards and a touchdown as the Redskins won, 23–21. They also won the following Sunday in Pittsburgh, 30–23, in Schroeder's first NFL start.

"On the opening kickoff, we ran it all the way back to the 1-yard line. So my first snap as a starting quarterback, I handed off [to George Rogers] for a touchdown," Schroeder said. "It was kind of fun. We were up 7–0 before I had to do anything. It's a very good way to start."

The young quarterback who became experienced in a hurry, finished the year completing 112 of 209 passes for 1,458 yards with five touchdowns and five interceptions as Washington won four of its last five games en route to a 10–6 record. They, however, missed out on making the playoffs on the final day of the season.

Putting the fact that they failed to make the postseason aside, the five starts gave Schroeder a personal victory.

"It kind of gave me a confidence boost. It kind of gave everybody around me a confidence boost," said Schroeder. "There were a lot of questions on what was going to happen after Joe was done playing. Unfortunately, his injury came sooner than anybody anticipated. But I was fortunate that I had a great football team around me. So my part was limited in all that I had to do was my job. The other guys were very good at doing what they did, and that helped a great deal."

Both Sides of the Spotlight

For all intents and purposes, Jay Schroeder was given a surprise pop quiz in 1985 and, well, passed it as if he had studied the right chapter on his way to school that morning. After Washington's veteran quarterback Joe Theismann suffered a career-ending broken leg during a mid-November game against the Giants, Schroeder, who was in his second season, stepped onto the field and led the Redskins to a victory over their division rivals. They had the same result for four out of the final five games of the season.

Schroeder remained the first-string quarterback as Washington opened the 1986 season with a five-game win streak and 11 victories in its first 13 games. One of the games the Redskins won was against the San Francisco 49ers during a Monday night game on November 17, which coincidently was almost exactly one year to the day from when Theismann was hurt.

While practicing during the week leading up to the game, Schroeder had made a deal with his teammates. "The promise was if we went through the game without a sack or anything like that, I would take the entire team out for dinner. And we did it! I ended up buying the team an eight-course Italian dinner, with their wives and girlfriends, which was tremendous. It was fun to be able to do stuff like that," said Schroeder, who footed the bill for around 80 people. "As my career went along, I ended up taking linemen out all the time for different things. I just thought that was part of my job. I enjoyed being with the guys and I was fortunate that we could do that."

Schroeder did the other part of his job very well by setting team single-season records with 541 pass attempts, completing 276 for 4,109 yards and being selected to play in the Pro Bowl. The Redskins topped the Rams and Bears in the playoffs, making it to the NFC Championship Game, where they were shut out by the Giants.

"[Aside from losing in the conference title game], that was a great year," said Schroeder. "We threw the ball all the time, and that's what you like to do as a quarterback. We had great wide receivers and a great offensive line that could pass block tremendously. So we just threw the ball and had a lot of fun.

"Anytime you can spread the ball around to guys like Art Monk, Gary Clark, and Ricky Sanders, it's a lot of fun. I think everybody had a great year doing that. We enjoyed it a lot."

Even though Washington won the Super Bowl, the 1987 season was less enjoyable for the former UCLA football and baseball star. Not only did he go through a players' strike, he also was involved in a quarterback controversy with Doug Williams and was replaced as starter.

"It was frustrating because in the first game of the season [against Philadelphia on September 13], I separated my [passing] shoulder, which a lot of people forgot about. What happened is, I tried to come back way too soon after the strike, and my strength in my shoulder just wasn't there. So I struggled," Schroeder said. "I wanted to play and do well, there's no question about it, but it just wasn't happening. So Coach [Gibbs] decided to go with Doug. But a lot of people forget that I played a lot during that season [with 10 starts, completing 129 of 267 passes for 1,878 yards, with 12 touchdowns and 10 interceptions]. So I was still very much a part of that football team no matter what people try to say or do."

A Call That Certainly Paid Off

Not to suggest that Joe Gibbs kept a little black book, but when the Redskins decided to search for a backup quarterback who had proven himself to add to their roster heading into the 1986 season, the head coach knew from experience just whom to call.

Eight years earlier, in 1978, Gibbs was in Tampa Bay for his one and only season as its offensive coordinator. That was also the season that the Buccaneers drafted Doug Williams, a quarterback from Grambling, with their first-round pick. The two would work closely together during that 5–11 campaign.

While Gibbs moved on to San Diego as an assistant coach and then to Washington, Williams spent four more seasons in Tampa Bay before a salary dispute with the team resulted with his playing for Oklahoma and Arizona in the USFL for two years before the league folded. And with no NFL teams knocking on his door, Gibbs' call could not have come at a better time.

"I got into [that first Buccaneers training] camp late, and he took an awful lot of time with me. I used to go to Coach Gibbs' house at night after practice," Williams said. "I think as a player, it has to be a professional relationship, and we both made an impact on each other. If we didn't, I don't think he would have gave me an opportunity to come to Washington."

Certainly appreciative of the opportunity to join the Redskins, Williams knew that his position would be as a second-stringer to Jay Schroeder. But having been a starter all his life, was there a chance that he'd become frustrated in his role?

"It wasn't frustrating at all. I came in there under the pretense that I was the backup. When Joe called, that was one of the discussions that we had. He told me that Schroeder was the [starting] quarterback and he just asked me, could I be the backup? And I'd never been a backup, so I do think that you have to ask a guy who has never been a backup whether or not, mentally, he can do it. But remember, when Joe called me, I didn't have a job. So it wasn't hard [to accept being second-string] at all."

Williams attempted just one pass that season. It was, however, a different story in 1987. In the season opener against the division-rival Philadelphia Eagles on September 13, he came in when Schroeder was injured and piloted the Redskins to a 34–24 victory. Two months later, on November 15 against Detroit, Williams came into the game in relief of a struggling Schroeder, and tossed a pair of touchdown passes to lead Washington to a 20–13 win.

And in his second of two starts that season, against Minnesota in the regular-season finale, he hit Ricky Sanders on two touchdown passes, including a 51-yard toss with less than two minutes left, to send the game into overtime. The Redskins would win it 27–24 to finish with an 11–4 record. Gibbs opted to keep Williams as the starting quarterback throughout the playoffs, and he earned the Most Valuable Player award after a record-breaking performance in Super Bowl XXII against Denver.

An Unhurried Hike to the Huddle

Selected in the sixth round of the 1986 draft out of Washington State, quarterback Mark Rypien completed just one pass out of three attempts in limited playing time during the preseason. However, an injured knee diminished his chances of appearing on the waiver wire, and he instead spent the season on Washington's injured reserve.

During the 1987 preseason, he showed a little more promise and completed 8 of 14 passes for 145 yards. But after suffering a back injury in the finale against the Los Angeles Rams, he was once again placed on the season-long injured-reserve list. Instead of feeling sorry for himself, Rypien used those two seasons to learn the ropes of playing in the NFL with minimal pressure.

"I think one of the problems in today's game is the fact that guys are thrown into the fire right off the bat," said Rypien. "I was fortunate enough for those two years to sit and watch Jay Schroeder play one year and then, of course, the following year was the strike-shortened year with Jay and Doug [Williams]. And Doug led us to the Super Bowl.

"But really, to that point, most of my time was done with [assistant coach] Jerry Rhome at practice in between defensive periods, working on the different reads and the different systems we had. To just be like a sponge and absorb as much as I possibly could with the offense."

In 1988 it wasn't Rypien who was sidelined, but Williams. The Super Bowl XXII MVP underwent an appendectomy and the "third-year rookie" quarterback finally had an opportunity to see some playing time and would start in six games for the Redskins.

"Physically, I thought the game was a lot faster than I was ready for, but mentally, I knew I was prepared," Rypien said. "As an athlete, you have to adapt to the environment you're in, and I was fortunate enough to play well enough. What we did offensively and the group of guys that we had from a preparation standpoint, we were as good as there was. Our attention to detail was something that we covered every day and something that was important.

"And when free agency started, we were a group that stayed together off the field as well as on the field. I think that's what kind of set us apart and made it easy to go out there and play on Sundays. You knew everyone's background; you knew everyone was going to be prepared. And that enabled us to perform. It made it easier on me knowing that and that I could just go out there and utilize what we had personnel-wise to help win football games."

From Starting to the Sideline to Stardom

It's obvious that nothing was handed to Mark Rypien. The eighth quarterback taken in the 1986 draft, his first two seasons with the Redskins were spent on injured reserve before earning the starting job during the 1989 training camp.

But after eight games and developing a case of fumble-itis, head coach Joe Gibbs' prescription was to have Rypien watch from the sideline. The two-game benching worked. After returning to the field on November 26 against Chicago, he brought the RFK Stadium faithful to its feet by completing 30-of-47 passes for 401 yards and four touchdowns in the 38–14 win. He led Washington to four more straight victories to close out the season and finished the year with 3,768 passing yards, the second-highest total in the team's history to the 4,109 yards that Jay Schroeder totaled in 1986.

Rypien's encore occurred two seasons later in 1991, when he had a career-high 28 touchdown passes, guided the Redskins to a 14–2 record and the Super Bowl XXVI title, and was named NFC Player of the Year.

"[That season's success] was a combination of things," said Rypien. "Knowing that the previous season I had an opportunity to play and win a playoff game on the road in Philadelphia, I felt from a standpoint of taking that next step, that from that point on if I was going to be a part of this organization, I needed physically and ability-wise to step up and answer the call.

"I didn't put a lot of pressure on myself, but I knew that this was going to be a big year. It was kind of one of those years where you look back on and it wasn't anything I did different. I made a lot of plays and did a lot of real good things up to that point in time. I'd made some mistakes when I was young and that was attributed to being a young player. But for the most part, I made a lot of plays, and that's what kept me in Joe Gibbs' graces.

"The fact [is] that it was hard for me to get out of the lineup because for the one or two things I did not do so well in a game, I'd come and do eight or 10 real good things. I just knew that I needed to be a little more consistent about everything I did and through it all, that's what happened in '91. The consistency came along with the big play, and that enabled us to get where we had gotten."

It's a What-Have-You-Done-Lately? World

Only two seasons after leading the Redskins to the Super Bowl XXVI championship and being named as the game's MVP, as well as the NFC MVP, quarterback Mark Rypien had a challenging year in 1993. Injuries caused him to miss four games during Richie Petitbon's one and only season as the head coach. And only Cincinnati had a worse record than Washington's 4–12 mark. "It was difficult for a couple reasons. I came back from an injury during the season, and hindsight would have indicated what happened afterward," said Rypien. "You make your decision based on the guys you go to war with each and every day. I got banged around that year and came back when I shouldn't have.

"But you're a struggling team and you see your guys out there, the same guys that were predominantly the guys that were in uniform with you on Super Bowl Sunday out there struggling. So you say to yourself, 'Gosh, I'm not in there. We're not doing very well. I need to come back.' So you do. You come back early and don't play well. Because of that, they think your days are numbered, and that's one of the knocks you get. When you play injured, you're not playing as well, but you're doing it for the right reasons. And I wouldn't change that ever."

Following the season, the veteran quarterback remembers being approached by representatives of the team's management about his contract. "Basically [because of] the [salary] cap number, they come to you and say, 'We'd still love to have you as part of the Redskins and this is the number we think you're worth now.' And you think of all the days you've been out there and spilled your guts. Even at that point in time, if I would have known what the future was, it wouldn't have been a bad thing to stick around, be a backup, be a tutor to Gus Frerotte, spend my last five, six, seven years there and then call it quits.

"Who knows? You might say that. But you also know what you have done and what you have accomplished and the effort that you put into it to get that. You remember your early years when you did a lot of good things, but never got rewarded for it. And you remember the great things you did and you finally got rewarded for it. Then they want to take that reward away from you. You say to yourself, 'No! I don't think that's right!' But that's just personal and it's a hard thing."

Rypien chose to sign elsewhere and joined the Cleveland Browns.

chapter 6

Moving the Chains

Running with the Boss

Don Bosseler left college football riding on a huge wave of momentum. The Miami running back had 28 carries for 189 yards in the 1957 Senior Bowl and was named as the game's Most Valuable Player. That recognition, doubled with what he had done on the field for the Hurricanes, added up to not lasting too long during the NFL Draft.

Chosen ninth overall in the opening round by the Redskins, Bosseler was actually the fourth running back taken off the board behind Notre Dame's Paul Hornung, who was the league's "bonus choice" and picked by Green Bay; Syracuse's Jim Brown, who was selected by Cleveland; and Clarence Peaks, who was nabbed by Philadelphia.

"That by itself made me feel pretty good. It was grand company," laughed Bosseler. "Back then, the draft wasn't as [publicized] as it is today. There wasn't any meeting place as they meet today in New York City, or all the scouting that goes on. I was contacted by various clubs by phone."

Bosseler reported to the team's training camp at Occidental State Teachers College near Pasadena, California, with a mixture of excitement and nervousness. "I really didn't know what to expect," he said. "Getting out there and looking at the guys coming in and not knowing what to expect, not knowing what type of practices and so on and so forth, I was not scared, but a little bit wondering what's going to happen."

What did happen was that Bosseler became an integral part of coach Joe Kuharich's offense and led Washington with 673 yards, the highest total since Rob Goode gained 951 yards six years earlier. Two seasons later, Bosseler averaged more than five yards per carry, put up 644 yards, and was named to the Pro Bowl. The team, however, won only three of its 12 games.

"We ran such a crazy offense the first couple of years," Bosseler said. "We ran an unbalanced line, which means there was either an extra guard or tackle over on the strong side. It wasn't an easy system because if I was left in the backfield to block, I had a big defensive end to block or a linebacker that had momentum coming. You don't want to do that all afternoon, let me tell you."

Bosseler and his teammates, not to mention the Redskins fans, endured many long afternoons during the immediate future. That was evidenced by the 1960 and '61 teams finishing with one-win records.

"Anytime you have a losing season, it's terribly frustrating. Basically, you feel sorry for the coaches. They're doing their best," Bosseler said. "The owner that we had at that time, George Preston Marshall, was not an easy person to get along with, so it made it extra tough.

"We used to get paid in cash on our day off, Monday. We'd have to go down to the Redskins office and kind of wait in line to talk with the accountant. I always pretty much had a standing note there from Marshall. It said, 'Make sure you see me before you leave this office!' The first time I got that, I was scared silly. I didn't know what he wanted. I didn't know what I did or did not do.

"Anyway, he kind of took a liking to me for whatever reason. I remember one time he called me in and said, 'Bosseler, sit down. You go back to Miami during the off-season, right?' I said, 'Yes.' He said, 'Do you read the papers down there? For crying out loud, you know I'm down there, so give me a call and come on over for lunch!' So I called him one given day and had lunch with him and [radio and television personality] Arthur Godfrey. It was an interesting conversation, I'll tell you that."

Lessons from Lombardi

When Washington's 1969 training camp opened under new head coach Vince Lombardi, that year's eighth-round draft choice, Larry Brown, admits that he was a little intimidated—and it wasn't because he was

Running back Larry Brown spent his entire eight-year career with the Redskins and won the NFL MVP Award in 1972.

worried about making the team, having been the third running back the Redskins selected.

Lombardi's legend made Brown nervous—even more so after he felt he was wrongly scolded for fumbling the ball during a scrimmage. "I think what was going through his head was, 'I have to make sure that Larry doesn't develop a cloud over his head that's so big that it would have an adverse effect on his personality,'" said Brown. "And he was looking for a way to, I guess, chastise or ridicule me in front of the team.

"And on this particular play, I did not fumble. I got up and laid the ball down. But I must have done it so quickly that it looked like I may have been separated from the ball while falling. So he said something to me, and I don't think I handled it very well. I may have said something back, and he may have threatened me in front of the team to the extent that he would not only run me out of the Washington Redskins organization, but out of the NFL, as well. Which clearly redefined the word *powerful* for me."

With clearly no question of who was in charge, Lombardi gave the rookie unique instructions on how to learn to handle the pigskin. "He made me carry a football everywhere I went for a week," Brown said. "That became a little embarrassing. And so because of that, you're the brunt of many jokes. He used peer pressure to kind of bring you in line because no one would like to go through the humiliation of carrying a football around everywhere you go; supermarkets, church, etc. It doesn't look very well, and you don't feel very well doing it."

As training camp continued, Lombardi seemed to notice that Brown was not hearing that well, either. "He kept asking me during the time that we were reviewing films of practice, 'Why are you constantly late getting off the ball?' You would not know that unless you slowed the film down, but he detected it," said Brown. "I told him that I was trying to determine the defensive alignment and therefore make sure it's adjusted to my role in a way so that I can carry out my assignment. That lasted for about three days. In other words, he accepted that for about three days.

"The next thing I know, there are about three people approaching me at my locker in long white coats. I didn't know what that was all about. All I was thinking was mental institution or something like that. I was trying to determine what I could have done to deserve this kind of treatment. I learned very shortly thereafter that they were there to give me a hearing examination, which confirmed that I was completely deaf in one ear."

With a hearing aid mounted inside his helmet and much keener awareness of the importance of hanging onto the ball, Brown played very well during his first season. He gained 888 yards on 202 carries—the highest totals by a Redskins running back since Rob Goode in 1951—was chosen to play in the first of four consecutive Pro Bowls, and finished second to Dallas' Calvin Hill for the league's Rookie of the Year Award.

Player of the Year

Playing under a third head coach in four seasons, Larry Brown was playing under a third offensive philosophy, as well. In 1972, his second year with George Allen patrolling the sideline, the fourth-year running back had a season to remember.

Helping the Redskins win 11 of their first 12 games en route to an NFC-best 11–3 mark, Brown found the end zone a dozen times, had six 100-yard games, and led the conference in rushing with a team-record 1,216 yards.

"In order to be competitive in this game, you always take every game at a time and you're always thinking about doing your best and giving 100 percent," said Brown, who set a team record by rushing for 191 yards against the Giants on October 29. "I didn't ever want to turn in a report prior to a game that ultimately would give the coach evidence that I didn't prepare well. And they could determine that by how well you kept meeting notes. You got graded! I never wanted to be embarrassed by getting a low grade in anything I did, be it blocking or running. I played every game as if I was expecting a good performance by myself.

"In my mind, that's what I wanted to accomplish. Not only just accomplish that, but in a winning team effort. And fortunately for me, that's what happened."

Totaling 101 yards on the ground versus Green Bay and 88 yards versus Dallas in the playoffs, Brown helped Washington earn the NFC title and meet Miami in Super Bowl VII. He also earned the league's Player of the Year recognition.

"I was deeply moved by that because I think that's probably one of the greatest honors one can get in this game," Brown said. "I was fortunate to get it [because] I sat out two games because of injuries."

Riggins Arrives

Although George Allen was widely known as a defensive-minded head coach, even he would not miss an opportunity to add another 1,000-yard running back to Washington's roster to go along with veterans Larry Brown and Calvin Hill. Even if it meant cutting short a family vacation in Paris, France, by two days.

Bonjour, John Riggins!

Having enjoyed his most productive season as a New York Jet with 1,005 yards in 1975, the sixth-year veteran had had enough of the big city, bright lights, and very few victories. Not once during his five

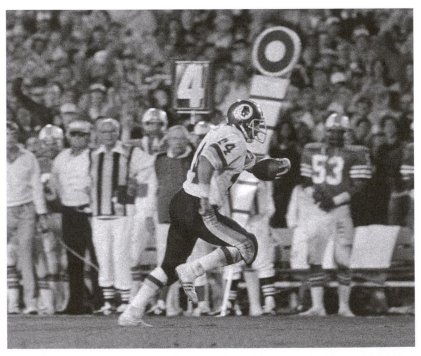

John Riggins rushed for 166 yards to push the Redskins past the Miami Dolphins in Super Bowl XVII.

seasons with the Jets did they ever post a winning record. Signing as a free agent with the Redskins in June 1976, he was joining a team that had had five consecutive winning seasons and had been in the playoffs four times.

"For a couple years there, I played the game without a heart," said Riggins. "It being a professional game, it seemed like I could do it that way. I was wrong and I apologized to the team for it."

Following the 1975 campaign, he had also gone to the team and reportedly asked to be paid the same per year as Jets star quarterback Joe Namath—$450,000. "The [salary] demand I put on the Jets was just my way of saying, 'It's been nice,'" said Riggins.

As a free agent, the 6'2", 230-pound Riggins, who was a straight-ahead runner and rock solid blocker, had the chance to receive a nice pay raise. However, he said money wasn't why he chose to sign with the Redskins over the three other teams that were pursuing him the most: the Los Angeles Rams, Houston Oilers, and Minnesota Vikings. "All things considered," he said, "I'd just as soon make Washington my home."

Regardless of where he chose to live around the city, Riggins was moving into a crowded backfield. In addition to Brown and Hill, who had signed as a free agent from Dallas, Washington also had second-year halfback Mike Thomas, who had rushed for 919 yards in 1975; Moses Denson, the incumbent starting fullback; and Ralph Nelson on their roster of running backs.

The competition did not concern the newest Redskin. "I'm just here to make the team," said Riggins. "I feel like a senior in high school getting ready to go to the big university and make my way in life."

24 Touchdowns!

Sure, he was the MVP of Super Bowl XVII after leading the Redskins past Miami to close the 1982 campaign. But even with 1980 as a one-year sabbatical due to a contract dispute, 1983 was, after all, his 12th season in the NFL.

How many running backs, particularly ones who give and take so many bone-cracking hits on the field, reach their peak after that many seasons? The *Jeopardy* response would be, "Who is John Riggins, Alex?"

After dropping the season opener to Dallas, 31–30, the Redskins rattled off five consecutive victories. The fifth occurring on October 9 in St. Louis, when Riggins, despite sitting out the fourth quarter, carried the ball 22 times for 115 yards and found the end zone three times.

Six games later, the Redskins traveled to Los Angeles to meet the NFC West–leading Rams on November 20. It must have been an off year for that division since Washington hammered the hosts, 42–20.

And even with an un-Riggins-like 78 yards on 22 carries; he again scored three touchdowns, breaking an NFL record by scoring a rushing touchdown in 12 consecutive regular-season games. He also tied Jim Taylor, Chuck Muncie, and Earl Campbell's NFL record of scoring 19 rushing touchdowns in a season.

However, after the game, he spoke about the Redskins' 10–2 record and their tie with the division rival Cowboys for the league's best mark, instead of his personal accomplishments.

"I was telling the guys on the sideline that I think we are on a collision course with Dallas," said Riggins. "We are a good enough team where we can play a waiting game and wait for the other team to self-destruct. The Rams did exactly that today.

"With the way the rules go now, it's really unfortunate. One team in our division will probably finish 14–2, the other 13–3. Some team will win its division with a 9–7 record and still get the home-field advantage, while the 13–3 team is the wild-card. That doesn't seem fair."

Riding an eight-game winning streak when they hosted the New York Giants in the season finale on December 17, Riggins, with 23 touchdowns, was tied with O.J. Simpson for the league's all-time single-season scoring record. The Giants did not make it easy. Washington fought to come from behind in the second half to win, 31–22, and wrap up the schedule with the NFC East title and a league-best 14–2 record.

Riggins, meanwhile, had 30 carries for a season-high 122 yards and scored on a two-yard run. He finished the year with a career-high 1,347 yards and an NFL-record 24 touchdowns. And for the only time in his career, he was named All-Pro. "Personally, I don't care to be remembered. Once you play, you play and that's it. I don't think you can pretend you're still a part of the game after you've left," Riggins said as the regular season was winding down. "You're talking about history. I really don't think that [my accomplishments] are so profound that they need to be labored, belabored, pondered, and remembered. I just don't think that it's that important.

"You see, I've gotten out of football what I've wanted. I've been as successful as I want to be. I really don't care to be a celebrity from football. After I leave the game and I'm 50 years old, I don't want to hear, 'John Riggins, wow, nice to meet you.' And I hope like hell that I don't need football to make people think I'm a decent man."

Stepping Out of the Shadows

Imagine that you're an astronaut and Neil Armstrong is your brother. Or that you're a talk show host and your sister is Oprah. Those are undoubtedly tough acts to follow.

Now you know what Keith Griffin had to deal with by having Archie, a two-time Heisman Trophy winner at Ohio State and a first-round draft choice of Cincinnati, and Ray, a second-round draft choice of the Bengals, as his older brothers.

It was both advantageous and challenging when he began his NFL career with Washington in 1984. "It was helpful in the sense that, growing up and watching them play, it helped me believe in myself and say, 'Hey, if they can do it, I can do it!' And then it hurt me in the sense of all the pressure of people watching me and trying to compare me to Archie," said Griffin, who was drafted in the 10th round out of Miami. "When I was growing up, people always asked my father, 'Who's going to be the best one?' He said, 'The little one here. He's going to be the best.' That tag sort of stayed with me.

"People were always watching, and they'd say they wouldn't put any pressure on you, but you were always thinking about it. So that's why I wanted to go somewhere and try to make a name for myself."

Because John Riggins was injured, Griffin's name was called to make his first start for the Redskins against Detroit 11 games into his rookie campaign. He gained 114 yards on 32 carries to help beat the Lions, 28–14.

"I was excited and had a lot of adrenaline flowing in me," Griffin said. "When I got the ball, I was just doing things naturally and I really wasn't thinking of things to do. I just got into the flow of the game. And I remember because I was small in stature, a defensive back came up to hit me, and I hit him! He got up and said, 'What you got under your shoulder pads?' That made me feel real good because I knew my style was to be aggressive and attack the defender as opposed to them attacking me. I wanted to gain respect from our opponent."

Just like the teammate he was stepping in for, Riggins. While Griffin had gotten advice from his brothers, he just had to observe the veteran to improve his performance.

"He was always prepared. Basically, by just watching him, it made me a better player in a sense that he had back pains at the time and he would go out there and play, give it his all," said Griffin, who rushed for 408 yards that season.

"I knew it before, but just to see someone be in traction all during the week and then come out and play.... I thought he was doing something great to be able to do that. He was dedicated to the game. I just said, 'Hey, he's hurt and gives 110 percent. I can do that at all times if I'm playing special teams or if I'm returning kicks or whatever.'"

Riggs' Record Is a Side Note

There is no question that Gerald Riggs set a very impressive all-time Redskins record on September 17, 1989. But it's unlikely that *impressive* would be the first word that comes to mind when describing all that came with his setting the mark.

Acquired in an April trade with the Falcons, the eighth-year veteran running back wanted to leave Atlanta after growing tired of rushing for high numbers only to see low numbers too frequently on the Falcons' side of the final score. In short, he wanted a change of scenery.

In his Redskins debut at RFK Stadium, the 1989 season opener against the Giants, Riggs once again put up a big number when he rushed for 111 yards. But Washington lost, 27–24, and Riggs uncharacteristically fumbled the ball twice.

A week later against Philadelphia, he broke George Rogers' team record for the most yards in a single game when he carried the ball 29 times for 221 yards. Unfortunately for Washington, the Superman-like performance came with a little kryptonite in the form of an untimely fumble.

After building a 20-point advantage over the Eagles in the first half, the Redskins saw that lead all but disappear in the closing minutes of the game. Philadelphia put together a 69-yard drive and found the end zone with 1:48 left to come within two points, 37–35.

And then during Washington's ensuing possession, Riggs had the longest run of his NFL career—58 yards—that put the ball at the Eagles' 22-yard line with 1:30 remaining. However, three plays later, while trying to run time off the clock, Riggs collided with one of the Hogs, Raleigh McKenzie, and the ball was knocked into the hands of Eagles linebacker Al Harris. He lateraled to his free safety, Wes Hopkins, who returned the ball 77 yards down the sideline to set up Philadelphia's game-winning touchdown—a four-yard pass from Randall Cunningham to tight end Keith Jackson. The final score: Eagles 42, Redskins 37.

Riggs may have put his name atop the all-time list for yards by a Redskins running back in only his second game with the team, but he could not have cared less. The way that Washington lost, four second-half turnovers, upset him enough that he waited a day to talk about the game, not the record. "I didn't remember anybody hitting me on the arm. I know at the time, I could feel the contact," said Riggs. "I was getting up the field, and it's a natural reaction to squeeze the ball. And before I could do it, it came out. I was like, 'Gosh, maybe it just slipped or hit my leg or something.' But I'm not gonna say just because [McKenzie] bumped me or something, I lost the ball.

"It just happened. It's one of those things. I just don't understand it. I can't put it on a slump or anything. I can't put my finger on it. Well, I better put my hand on it."

A Fresh Start

Traded to the Redskins on the 1989 draft day, running back Earnest Byner arrived from Cleveland with five years of experience under his belt and the massive weight of countless Browns fans on his shoulders.

Despite totaling 2,713 rushing yards, 2,034 receiving yards, and 31 touchdowns, Byner's legacy in Cleveland was shadowed by a late-game fumble at the 3-yard line as he was going for a tying touchdown against Denver in the AFC Championship Game on January 17, 1988. The Broncos advanced to Super Bowl XXII and were ripped by the Redskins, 42–10.

And while Byner felt some anxiety over the trade, he looked forward to a bright beginning in Washington. "I was starting over again," said Byner. "Basically, after I got down there, I felt like I had to prove myself all over again. So I looked at it like I was a rookie. And actually, I felt like I was a rookie in that circumstance and situation."

After scoring nine touchdowns for the Redskins, if it had been his first season, Byner would have been a favorite to collect Rookie of the Year honors. "I think the coaching staff understood some of the things I could do," he said, "and what I brought to the table, but I don't think that they really, fully thought that I'd ever become the running back that I did for the team. Especially in consideration of them bringing in Gerald Riggs on the same day!

"I was more of an H-back type of player, a third-down guy. As a matter of fact, I think if Kelvin Bryant hadn't gotten hurt, that wouldn't have matured as it did. But I think the initial thing that happened was that they wanted to see me prove myself to them and also to the guys. I think when I did that, the fans said, 'Well, who is this guy?'"

That wasn't even a question the following season. Stepping to the forefront of Washington's ball-control offense, Byner finished fourth in the NFL in rushing with 1,219 yards and was selected to play in the Pro Bowl.

"I never had any doubt as far as my capability of running the ball and also being a featured back," Byner said. "The 1,200 yards is a by-product of having a good line and also having some overall toughness and skills that probably people didn't think I had.

"[Being named to the Pro Bowl roster] was very gratifying because I felt like I had played good enough a couple of years in Cleveland to be there, but [Browns teammate] Kevin Mack went instead [along with] some other guys in the AFC. Being respected like that by your peers definitely puts a stamp that you have reached the pinnacle of the game."

He reached it again in 1991 en route to helping the Redskins capture the Super Bowl XXVI championship.

A Pick Helped by Past Performances

If running back Ricky Ervins' junior season at USC, when he led the Pac-10 in rushing with 1,395 yards and was named the MVP of the Rose Bowl, had actually been his senior campaign, which ended in the fourth game because of an ankle injury, chances are great that he wouldn't have been available when the Redskins chose him in the third round of the 1991 draft.

But he was.

"I was happy just to be drafted, period," said Ervins. "I wasn't sure if I was going to be or not because of missing damn near the whole season. I think at the [scouting] combine and the all-star games, I picked my stock back up."

But when the NFL held the draft on April 21, he had no assurances. And so between seeing where his future in football would be and well, homework, it turned out to be a long day.

"I was working on a paper that was due," Ervins said, "The [television] coverage came on at 9:00 [in the morning] and went off at 3:00. The first two rounds were so long, though, it took up all the [broadcast] time, and they didn't have any room for the other rounds. So I figured once they took the coverage off, they'd just start picking [more quickly]. I didn't get no calls until 6:30, and I was actually kind of asleep. It was [Washington's general manager] Charley Casserly, and he said, 'We're thinking about picking you in the next round. I'll call you back in two minutes.'

"By that time, I was happy somebody called. But at the same time, I was thinking they might pick somebody else. So I just sat there by the phone, and it actually rang twice. One, my sister called. I was like, 'Why in the hell are you calling me?'" laughed Ervins. "And then they called."

Ervins was the only running back the Redskins called during the two-day draft to announce he'd been selected. He was joining veterans Earnest Byner, Gerald Riggs, and Brian Mitchell. And fortunately for the rookie, they soon took him under their wings.

"Yeah, pretty much all of them did," Ervins said. "I'll say the one who really taught me a lot would be Earnest Byner. It's funny because I was naïve of players switching teams. When I saw him, I thought he was actually a coach. I didn't know who he was. In mini-camp, we were going through a couple drills against the linebackers, and he goes out on a route. I said, 'This guy actually plays?' I was just totally amazed with his route running. Brian Mitchell, also. With that being his second year, he showed me a lot, as well."

And with 680 yards rushing, 181 receiving yards, four touchdowns, and a 21-yard average on 11 kick returns during his first season, Ervins showed a lot, as well.

Davis' September to Remember

After filling in at fullback for an injured Larry Bowie in 1998, fourth-year veteran Stephen Davis was ready to return to the halfback position and carry the load for the Redskins in 1999. The only thing was that second-year running back Skip Hicks had the same idea.

"I knew that [Washington head coach] Norv Turner was a guy that liked to run the ball with different types of movements that he had in his offense," said Davis. "And my main concern was to just win the starting job because I was competing with Skip Hicks. I paid the dues and I did everything as far as to get me into that position to compete for the starting job."

Davis won the job and was in the starting lineup when Washington hosted Dallas in the season opener on September 12. He carried the ball 24 times for 109 yards and scored two touchdowns in the 41–35 loss.

The following week, the Redskins traveled to the New Jersey Meadowlands, a site where they had lost on five of their last six visits, to meet the New York Giants. Taking a 21-point lead in the opening quarter on three touchdown runs of 1, 1, and 19 yards by Davis, Washington won, 50–21. That was the team's highest total since scoring 56 against Atlanta on November 10, 1991. Davis finished with a game-high 126 yards on 23 carries. "The thing that I remember most is that our offensive line was blocking very well. And I know that we scored a lot of points," Davis said. "[One other] thing that I remember is that we were going for a first down on third-and-1 or fourth-and-1 and the whole Giants defense thought I was down, but I wasn't. I popped out to the left side and [ran 19 yards for a touchdown]."

The Redskins were back in the Meadowlands a week later on September 26 to play against the New York Jets. And even though Davis came up seven yards shy of cracking the century mark for a third consecutive game, he did find the end zone three more times to help Washington win, 27–20. "Going into that game I knew that [New York's running back] Curtis Martin was having a good year…and I just wanted to go out there and compete and do the best I can and basically show everybody what I could do," Davis said.

With 328 yards and eight touchdowns in the first three games, by the time the month of September came to an end, assuredly the rest of the NFL knew what Davis could do. And if they didn't, surely they did by the end of the season when he broke Terry Allen's team record with 1,405 yards. "Considering that the record I broke belonged to a guy that I looked up to, it was great," said Davis, who was selected to play in the Pro Bowl. "When I first got in the pros, he took me under his wing and taught me how to be a pro. He taught me the toughness of it, what it takes day in and day out, and how to use things to my advantage as far as my size and everything. And just being able to have the opportunity to do that and to go out there and do that in the fashion that I did was great."

chapter 7

Slants, Curls, and Going Deep!

Much More Than Just a Trade

Bobby Mitchell was much more than a halfback when the Redskins acquired him from Cleveland in 1962. He was a pioneer. Washington traded its rights to first-round draft choice Ernie Davis, the Heisman Trophy–winning running back from Syracuse, to the Browns for the four-year veteran and the rights to Cleveland's top draft pick, Leroy Jackson. The transaction made Mitchell and Jackson the first black men to ever play for the Redskins.

"[Cleveland's coach] Paul Brown wanted to trade for Ernie and, as it turned out, it seems I was one of the only guys [Redskins owner George Preston] Marshall said he would take," Mitchell wrote in *Hail Redskins*. "They didn't have any blacks on the team then, never had, and Marshall was told that if he didn't put some blacks on the team, they weren't going to play in the D.C. Stadium anymore. So I was the guy.

"I was on my way to Washington to begin what turned out to be a career with the Redskins [and] I was concerned. I was leaving a team that had been a real contender, always winning seasons, and joining one that had won only one game the year before, the worst record in the NFL. And a team that had never fielded a black player before."

Shortly after reporting to the team's training camp, Mitchell would be asked to do something that he had never done before—play as a

Receiver Bobby Mitchell racked up 14,078 net yards during his career and was inducted into the Pro Football Hall of Fame in 1983.

receiver. "I could tell they didn't have a lot of good ballplayers. I watched the [offensive] line, and as a running back I felt there was cause for some real concern. Coach [Bill] McPeak said to me, 'You can tell we don't have much of a line, but I've got a pretty good quarterback, Norm Snead. What would you think about playing outside?' I took another look at that line and said, 'Yup.'

"I'd never played as a receiver before, but I was sure I could do it. Throughout the training camp that summer I worked with Norm. There was no receivers coach in those days, so we just worked it out among ourselves, and by the time the season was ready to start we had connected pretty good."

After opening the 1962 season with a tie in Dallas, on September 23 the Redskins traveled to Cleveland, a city they had not won in since 1956, to play a team they had lost the last eight games to. Nevertheless, Mitchell was excited to be back in his old stomping grounds.

"I really wanted to do well against them," Mitchell wrote. "They were a big favorite that day, and I didn't get the ball as much as I would've liked, but I did get it in the end and scored the game-winning touchdown [in the 17–16 victory]. It was one of the most memorable moments of my career.

"Later that season the Browns came to Washington, and we beat them again [17–9]. Then the next year I caught a pass for a 99-yard touchdown [from George Izo] against the Browns [during a 37–14 loss], another moment I really cherish, which was a Redskins record [that's still shared]."

An Eventual Natural

Even though Charley Taylor was an All–Western Athletic Conference halfback as a senior at Arizona State and the Redskins' first-round draft choice in 1964, when he reported to Washington's training camp, head coach Bill McPeak told him that his role would be to back up the veterans. That didn't stay that way too long. "At the beginning I was going to be the No. 2 [halfback]," Taylor said. "Then in the preseason, a couple guys got hurt and I just sort of started developing. [And then] they traded [eight-year veteran and the team's leading rusher two of the previous three seasons] Dick James [to the New York Giants], so I felt I sort of had the job. I was just happy to make the team. They had some good players here."

Taylor could have included himself in that assessment, because to say the least, he had a good season. Earning the NFL's Rookie of the Year Award, he was Washington's leading rusher with 755 yards, the most by a Redskin since Rob Goode ran for 951 yards in 1951, and scored five touchdowns. Taylor added 53 catches, a record for running backs at that time and just seven fewer than the team's leading receiver, Bobby Mitchell, for 814 yards, and found the end zone five more times.

After leading the Redskins in rushing again in 1965, the following season new head coach Otto Graham, a Hall of Fame quarterback, moved Taylor to split end opposite of Mitchell in the seventh game, giving veteran quarterback Sonny Jurgensen another target and strengthening the team's passing attack. "I just wanted to play," recalls Taylor. "Really, being moved outside was cool, too. That was fine. Otto Graham made the move, and who was I to second-guess him?"

Good idea! During his first two seasons at the new position, Taylor led the NFL in receptions, became a regular in the Pro Bowl [being chosen eight times in all], and was arguably the best receiver in the league. That was despite playing for five different head coaches: McPeak, Graham, Vince Lombardi, Bill Austin, and George Allen. "Well, basically, they didn't have all these different West Coast offenses. So just the terminology was the main difference," Taylor said. "You still did the same thing. They all had different personalities, and you had to adjust to that. You have to grow when you go under too many different systems like that. I respected all the coaches and tried to fulfill what they thought they had planned. For a couple of them—it worked."

Taylor retired following the 1977 season as the NFL's all-time leading receiver at the time with 649 catches for 9,110 yards and 79 touchdowns. He was inducted into the Pro Football Hall of Fame in 1984.

A Trade Based on Integrity

Veteran receiver Roy Jefferson's belief that he got a raw deal in Baltimore led to a terrific deal for Washington. Following five seasons with the Pittsburgh Steelers, Jefferson was with the Colts during the 1970 campaign and was their leading receiver in the Super Bowl V victory over Dallas. However, in 1971 the two-time Pro Bowler was surprisingly acquired by the Redskins for rookie receiver Cotton Speyrer and a future draft choice.

"The problem was with [Colts owner] Carroll Rosenbloom," said Jefferson. "I had signed a three-year contract previous to my coming to Baltimore. And so when I got there, I asked for a meeting and told him that I had no problem playing under the first year of the contract, but I'm in a completely new situation. I want the opportunity that if I have a good season and the team has a good season, to come back in and renegotiate the last two years. He told me he had absolutely no problem with it."

Following the Super Bowl, Jefferson was in Los Angeles and came across an article in the local paper. The reporter had asked several coaches why the Colts had been so successful that season, and they each credited him with solidifying the passing game. Jefferson thought it would be beneficial in the upcoming contract talks and clipped the story to show the owner.

"I go back and take that to him, and he says to me that he never said he would renegotiate my contract," Jefferson said. "Right then I told him, 'Mr. Rosenbloom, you know what you said and I know what you said. And basically, you lied to me. I will never play for you again. I want to be traded.' And so I named four teams [Washington, Los Angeles, San Diego, and Minnesota] that I wanted to be traded to or I was going to retire."

And so, after reporting late to the following training camp and showing up to play in the annual Super Bowl champs versus college all-stars game just to prove he was healthy, Jefferson was sent to the Redskins and their first-year head coach George Allen.

"I was elated! [Allen] never really told me what my role would be," said Jefferson. "He just mentioned the fact that he enjoyed having experienced receivers. He was of a mind and expressed to me that based on my experience and my talent and background, that he was happy and most glad that he had me on his team."

After leading the Redskins in receiving with 47 catches for 701 yards and four touchdowns, Jefferson concluded his personally chaotic year by being selected to play in the Pro Bowl. "It verified to me that I was considered one of the top receivers in the league."

Warren's the Definition of Consistency

There have been some players in the NFL who, regardless of their talent level, would spell *team* with four *I*s if they could. They're the type who would call a press conference to announce that they were going to hold a press conference.

Don Warren was not such a player. Not even close. Actually, from the time he was selected by the Redskins in the fourth round of the 1979 draft to when he retired following the 1992 season, a 14-year career, the tight end from San Diego State took nothing for granted and humbly felt that he had to continually prove himself worthy of being on Washington's roster. "I did whatever I could to be the best player that I could because I don't think I had all that much talent," Warren said. "I had to work a lot harder to stay in the game and be consistent."

To have been able to play in 193 regular-season games for the Redskins, Warren was a model of consistency. But how did he do it? "I think there are three things. My work habits. No. 2 would be [Washington's longtime strength coach] Dan Riley, by keeping me going and in shape and as strong as he did throughout the years. And then the third thing was winning and actually going to four Super Bowls in those 14 years," said Warren, who wore the burgundy-and-gold uniform in three different decades.

"It just so happened that it got kind of spread out where I went to two early in my career [XVII in 1982, XVIII in 1983], one kind of in the middle [XXII in 1987], and one at the end [XXVI in 1991]. It's like you don't want to try to fix something that's not really broken. I think that really helped out, too. So those are the things that probably helped me last as long as I lasted."

Another reason why Warren may have enjoyed the longevity and success that he did is because of his teammates. While it is true that some of the faces changed from year to year, the unity of those who shared the locker room, the huddles, and the team goals, did not.

"It was really different than it is now. You had a lot more loyalty because guys were staying with one team a lot longer and not chasing the big dollars," Warren said. "Now you get a guy who plays for three years and then he's moving on to the next team. I think that's what really helped us out, helped us in the '80s to be such a winning team. We were able to keep our [offensive] line basically together, which as everybody sees now is really crucial.

"That and the type of personalities we had on the team. We just had blue-collar guys and we were all, you hate to say the old cliché that we were all family, but we really were. We really watched out for each other's back. It wasn't like we just went to practice and went home and treated it as a job. We had a lot of fun. After practice, we spent time with each other. We really knew each other, knew each other's wives and families. We really backed each other up, and I think that made a difference."

Modest Monk

As a receiver with the Redskins for 14 seasons, Art Monk was famously reserved as well as widely respected. He was not one who would toot his own horn during postgame press conferences. Actually, it is likely that his horn would not have seen the light of day outside of its case if it had been left up to him.

His abilities on the field, however, screamed greatness. Monk was as liable to catch a key pass as he was to lay down a key block. Win or lose, from 1980, when he was Washington's first-round draft choice out of Syracuse, until his final game with the team in 1993, Redskins fans witnessed a better game because Monk was wearing a burgundy-and-gold uniform.

Washington's all-time leading receiver with 888 catches for 12,026 yards, Monk found his way to the end zone 65 times. A three-time Pro Bowler, he was inducted into the Pro Football Hall of Fame in 2008 and talked about his Redskins days during the induction ceremony. "I've had some great teammates over the years, and obviously I wouldn't be here [without] them," Monk said. "We've worked hard. We've battled together. We've cried together. We shared some great times together. But

One of the greatest wide receivers in NFL history, Art Monk was inducted into the Pro Football Hall of Fame in 2008 alongside teammate Darrell Green.

there are a couple of teammates, groups of teammates that I would specifically like to mention who really made a difference for me.

"When I first arrived at the Redskins, there was a group of guys there known as the Over-the-Hill Gang. These were partially gray-haired, cigar-smoking, trash-talking veterans who were serious about their football and who played really hard. And because I was an incoming rookie, they gave me a hard time, physically and mentally, they tested me. Not just to see and to prove me worthy of wearing the burgundy and gold, but to see if I would be the type of player that would fit in to being a team player and one that they can trust and count on.

"These guys were also full of experience and wisdom and often they would pull me aside before practice, during practice, after practice, outside of practice, and give me valuable words of wisdom about myself as a person, my skill as a wide receiver, and about the game of football being played in Washington, D.C. I am grateful for those men. I've learned a lot from them. And they really helped set the ground work for the rest of my career.

"I'm close with a lot of my former teammates that really helped me along the way. But there's one specific group that has become like family to me. There's Monte Coleman, there's Charles Mann, there's Darrell Green, there's Tim Johnson and Ken Coffey. They're the ones who not only took the time to share the gospel to me, but they also demonstrated it in their lives, which allowed me to receive the gospel for myself. And this was a life-changing experience for me.

"From the time I first picked up a football, I fell in love with this game. It's all I ever wanted to do. From playing tackle in the streets of White Plains [New York] to playing in the stadiums in the NFL, I never, ever imagined it would take me this far. It's taken a lot of hard work and sacrifice and the belief from people and times when I didn't believe in myself. I've experienced some exciting moments. I've met some extraordinary people and I have a lot of great memories that I will never forget.

"This is the icing on the cake for me, and I take it very seriously. And I'm extremely honored to now be included with this group of elite athletes and to do so with my Class of 2008. I will wear the banner with pride. And I will represent it well."

"Doc" Finds a Home

Free agency could not have come soon enough for tight end Rick "Doc" Walker. After being drafted by the Bengals in 1977, the three seasons he spent with them were both figuratively and literally painful.

"I broke my arm twice my rookie year, dislocated my elbow my second [year], and in my third [season], it was a sprained neck and shoulder injury," said Walker, who missed 15 games due to injuries and experienced back-to-back 4–12 seasons in Cincinnati before he tried out as a free agent in Washington in 1980. "I had an injury grievance going, and I had to come in and work out for [general manager] Bobby Beathard and [head coach] Jack Pardee. I came in on a Thursday, and we played the Giants that Sunday [in the second game of the season on September 14]. I ended up playing a quarter and I remember [offensive tackles] Terry Hermeling, George Starke, [quarterback] Joe Theismann, and the guys telling where to go [on different plays]."

Walker and his teammates had to learn a whole new playbook the following season when Joe Gibbs succeeded Pardee as the head coach of the Redskins. And even though they were a middle-of-the-road 8–8 team in 1981, the tight end sensed that the team was moving to the NFL highway's passing lane and heading for success. "That was the team that started off 0–5 and was able to right itself and get on a roll," Walker said. "We lost a game [on November 29] up in Buffalo [21–14, after winning five out of the previous seven games]. If we'd won that, we were 9–7 and went to the playoffs. I thought that really kind of weeded out the people that weren't going to be here and started to establish a platform for the way the offense would go. The defense and special teams was always—we always led with special teams, so that was a no-brainer."

The 1982 season was a test that the Redskins passed with hardly any difficulty. A strike shortened the campaign to just nine games. And if the Redskins had not stuck together as a team, they would not likely have won eight of them. They would not likely have beaten Dallas for the NFC championship. And they almost certainly would not have beaten the Miami Dolphins in Super Bowl XVII.

"That season starts off and we go 2–0 and then the strike [happened]," said Walker. "The nucleus of guys, about 48, stayed in town. We lifted [weights] together and worked out over in Herndon, where we ran our offense against our defense and just did about everything but had coaches and contact.

"We were able to get through that and come back and hit the ground running [to win six out of the last seven games]. We were just better...at that point and played real hard."

Not Anonymous for Long

Sure, Clint Didier may have been the 314th player selected in the 1981 NFL Draft, but look at it this way: how many eligible college players were not chosen at all?

The Portland State tight end, who was picked in the 12th round, traveled to Washington with nothing to lose. And at the very least he'd have a good story to tell his grandchildren someday.

"I wasn't really intimidated, I was more in awe," said Didier. "I remember my first walk through the locker room. I was by myself and I was just in awe of the names above the lockers. But the thing that struck me the most was the ashtrays in some of the lockers. I couldn't believe it! Here were some of these primo athletes, and they smoked cigarettes! It just didn't seem like it could fit together. It just amazed me that there was somebody that could smoke and go out and play a football game."

In an ironic twist, what occurred soon thereafter was also health-related. Didier pulled a hamstring during training camp and was actually summoned to the league's headquarters to be examined by one of their physicians. "[Rookie quarterback] Phil Kessel and I went to New York and we had to get okayed that we had legit injuries," Didier said. "This was before practice teams and this was a way for teams to hide players. But our injuries were legit. I had a hamstring pull that didn't get well until after I had a shot of cortisone in it. And that needle was about as long as you can imagine. It was about six inches long, but of course, your memory always makes it bigger than it was. They hit my sciatic nerve when they injected my hamstring, and that brought me right off the table. But it cured it. When I got healthy, I was a practice-team player, just like they have today.

"The pressure was still there because you had to keep yourself energized. There were no coaches even talking to you. You were a being in the locker room, you were a being in the facility, and you weren't treated with respect because you weren't really a part of the team. You were just there serving out a year of learning.

"That year of experience that I gained from the athletes that were there was crucial in my making the team the next year. And I'll tell you, it made me hungry! I came home and worked out the hardest I ever worked out. I went back and out-tested almost the whole team in mini-camp. That was just a big-time rush and confidence-builder when [the coaches] started showing enthusiasm and interest in me. There was a spark there, and that lit the fire. That year of experience was critical in my making the team and being a part of the Washington Redskins."

The tight end spent the next six seasons with the team, hauling in 129 passes and finding the end zone 19 times. Didier went from an anonymous guy in the locker room to Washington's leading receiver in Super Bowl XVIII.

The Fourth Time Is the Charm

Years from now when Ron Middleton sits down with his grandchildren and tells them about how he became a member of the Redskins, hopefully they will have packed a lunch and taken a nap, because it's going to take a while.

Okay, here goes. After two seasons of playing tight end for the Atlanta Falcons, he signed as a free agent with Washington in 1988. He was then waived. However, he signed with the Redskins again later that season and played on special teams in two games. But then he was waived again. He re-signed with the Redskins for the 1989 training camp and would then be waived by them for the third time.

Middleton then signed with the Tampa Bay Buccaneers and was cut. On to Cleveland, where he played in nine games for the Browns and caught three passes, including a three-yard touchdown against Buffalo during an AFC playoff game.

And then shortly before the 1990 draft, the Redskins took out their Rolodex, stopped at the *M*s and called about signing Middleton for a fourth time.

"It was unbelievable! I talked to my agent, and he told me told me, 'The Redskins have called and they were asking about you.' I said, 'Well, hang up on them! I don't want to talk with them,'" said Middleton. "He said, 'No, you might want to listen to what they're saying.' So I did. I talked with Coach [Joe] Gibbs, and he basically told me, and then he said it to the media, they made a mistake by letting me go the year before and they'd like to have me back. So I came back and I'm glad I did."

It's fair to say the Redskins were glad, as well. After making five starts at H-back that season, Middleton had 12 starts at tight end in 1991 and helped them compile a 14–2 record, the best mark in the team's history.

"We had some pretty big injuries at the beginning of the year. [Veteran tight end] Donny Warren blew his ankle out during camp, and I was blessed and fortunate enough to be able to step in," Middleton said. "Our whole offensive line stayed intact just about the whole year. We got some continuity offensively and defensively and we really came together as a team."

So much so that Washington earned the Lombardi Trophy after beating Buffalo in Super Bowl XXVI.

Not Much Middle Ground

During a span of less than three seasons, tight end Ron Middleton had the opportunity to experience three different head coaches and three different personalities. In 1992, his fourth year with the Redskins, Middleton suited up one last time for Hall of Famer Joe Gibbs.

"He was very organized and he was hard-nosed and believed in hard work, and that's what I pride myself on, being organized and prepared," said Middleton. "I think Coach Gibbs was an honest man, and that's still hard to find this day in the NFL. I really respect him a lot."

With 24 receptions for 154 yards and two touchdowns, Middleton enjoyed his finest year stat-wise in 1993 under Gibbs' replacement Richie Petitbon. Unfortunately for both of them, it was also their final season in Washington.

"Transitional-wise, as far as procedure and everything, it was basically the same. Richie had been there, if I'm not mistaken, the whole time that Coach Gibbs had been there. So the blueprint was set. The difference with Richie's year [was] we were just decimated by injuries. We pulled guys off waivers on Tuesday, and they'd be starting on Sunday.

"On the offensive line, for sure. Raleigh McKenzie and myself were the only two guys that started every game that year. It doesn't matter what level you're playing on if you don't have any continuity and you're trying to mix it as you go.... It was just unbelievable the amount of injuries we had that year." The injury-attacked Redskins finished the campaign under Petitbon with a 4–12 record. He was fired and followed in 1994 by Norv Turner.

"I got injured right before training camp," Middleton said. "I had a severely pulled hamstring and I missed a lot of [practices]. Norv Turner said all along, 'Take it slow. Take it slow. [From] watching last year's tape, you can play for my team anytime. As long as I'm here, you can play for my team.' But then I tried to come back too early, and he basically just got me on [video] tape [showing I was not injured enough to stay off the field] so they could cut me. Easy to say, I'm not a big Norv Turner fan."

chapter 8

Owning the Line of Scrimmage

Death, Taxes, and Hauss at Center

Beginning in 1964 after he was drafted out of Georgia and for the next 14 seasons, there was a better chance that a coin flip would not come up either heads or tails than there was that Len Hauss would not be on the field for the Redskins.

From the season opener of his rookie year until the 1977 season finale—a span of 196 regular-season and seven postseason games—he was in Washington's lineup at center. He was in the starting lineup for 192 consecutive games.

"There were times I was told I should not play [because of injuries]. But most, I guess, all of the times I was told, 'But it's up to you.' So if it were up to me, my decision would be, if I can play, I play," said Hauss, who played well enough to be named to six consecutive Pro Bowls. "Sort of the way it worked was if you can't practice Wednesday or Thursday, then you can't play on Sunday. I guess generally there was an exception made for a lot of us. I guess the worst thing I ever played with was two broken thumbs. One [occurred] one week and one the following week. They were fractured, but I could still handle the ball."

That was fortunate for the other men wearing the burgundy-and-gold uniforms. An enormous majority of the time that quarterbacks Sonny Jurgensen and Billy Kilmer and running backs Larry Brown and John Riggins looked through their face masks across the huddle, they'd see Hauss. And whenever one of them made a big play, he'd have something to do with that, as well. Hauss was the consummate teammate.

"You kind of have to understand the game pretty well, but every record that Sonny holds for the Redskins, every record that Larry holds, every record that Jerry Smith, Charley Taylor, Bobby Mitchell holds, I snapped the ball. Every one of their superior days was a superior day for me."

Rand McNally & Starke

George Starke did not need a playbook when he began—scratch that—when he tried to begin a career in the NFL. He needed a road map.

And actually, had he not been so excited about his gridiron future, the Columbia tight end may have had an inkling that he was going to have an unusual journey the evening before the 1971 draft. "I talked with George Allen the night before, and he said he was going to become the Redskins' new coach, but he didn't need a tight end. They had a pretty good one there, and he was right, they had Jerry Smith," said Starke. "He said could I play any other position than tight end? And being the quick-thinking man that I was, I said, 'Probably offensive tackle.' Which I had not played! And he said, 'Okay,' hung up the phone, and the next day I was drafted in the 11th round by the Washington Redskins as an offensive tackle."

Starke's burgundy-and-gold uniform days were short-lived. Less than three weeks after reporting to Washington's training camp in Carlisle, Pennsylvania, he was waived by Allen and claimed by Kansas City Chiefs head coach Hank Stram.

"He wanted me to get to Kansas City as quickly as possible [because] he needed a tackle and a tight end. So I jumped in my car and drove from Carlisle to Kansas City and finished out the 1971 training camp with the Chiefs. And then I got cut just before they opened the season on September 19. But Hank asked me to stay in Kansas City and [told me] that he would eventually get me on the roster, which in fact did not happen.

"So while I was still in Kansas City trying to figure out how to get back to New York for Christmas, there was a knock on my door. It was a little man with a big hat. He said, 'Hello, I'm from the Dallas

Cowboys. We've been looking for you.' [It turned out that] every time they called Hank, Hank would say he didn't know where I was. Hank was both not paying me and wouldn't let anyone else have me. So, anyway, he asked me to go to training camp with the Cowboys in 1972, which in fact, I did."

Starke continued. "I was there for a couple months, got released by the Cowboys, and picked up again by the Redskins. So I came back to Washington and was on the taxi squad for half the year, then got hurt in practice and spent the rest of '72 on injured reserve, which of course is the year the Redskins went to the Super Bowl [VII]."

His perseverance paid off in 1973 when he became Washington's starting right tackle. And even more so when you consider that he would remain with the Redskins for the next 11 seasons.

A Strong Second Half

Center Len Hauss feels that his 14-year career with the Redskins had a halftime. The first seven seasons, 1964 through 1970, he refers to as "Before George." That's when he played for four head coaches—Bill McPeak, Otto Graham, Vince Lombardi, and Bill Austin—and experienced only one winning season, the 1969 campaign under Lombardi when the team went 7–5–2.

"After George" began in 1971 with the arrival of his fifth and last head coach—George Allen, who most recently had been with the Los Angeles Rams. Allen brought a new attitude and a number of experienced players to Washington, which concerned Hauss and some of the other veterans who were already there. "A number of us that had been starters for a number of years thought maybe he was getting too heavy with [former] Rams," said Hauss. "We used to kid about being the 'Ramskins.'"

Hauss' concern about the infiltration into the locker room would subside, however, after conversations with his new coach grew into a relationship of mutual respect. "He made me think that I was part of his plan. I was a little bit outspoken and I think he probably appreciated that because if you've studied him closely, you'll know that he emphasized defense. And if you weren't careful, the offense would get lost in the shadows. I think I helped keep the offense as out-front as we were, at least keep the offense visible. Often times, I felt like I might have gone too far. But I think he respected that aspect of it."

Hauss learned to enjoy the aspect of winning games. During Allen's first season on the sideline, the Redskins posted a 9–4–1 record and made the playoffs for the first time since 1945. They won 11 of 14 games the following year, beat Dallas for the NFC championship, and played in Super Bowl VII against Miami. "The time after the Cowboys game," says Hauss, "when we realized we were going to the Super Bowl, that was probably as high as any of us from that era ever felt."

Future Helped with a Map

Just suppose for a moment that after he was released by the Eagles late in the 1980 training camp, rookie free agent center Jeff Bostic had decided to go sightseeing in New York for a few days before he headed home.

He, however, chose to forgo the opportunity to tour the Empire State Building and, as an indirect result, would spend the next several seasons in another tourist-rich city.

"The Redskins had shown interest before I signed to go to Philadelphia. So I was heading back to North Carolina and I figured Washington's right on the way, so I went by and worked out for them," said Bostic. "I didn't realize a lot of the problems they were having, but it seemed like a punt snap had gone over the punter's head every game in the preseason. I ran and did all these little drills, and they basically told me, 'If we have any more problems, we're going to call you.' So I headed back home and watched the Redskins' [final preseason] game on TV, and on the first [punt] snap of the game, the ball goes sailing over the punter's head! The next day, I got the call."

After high-tailing it back to Washington, Bostic signed with the Redskins as a long-snapper less than a week before the season opener against Dallas on September 8. He went through that game and the rest of the schedule without making any bad snaps and was awarded a game ball from head coach Jack Pardee for causing a fumble during the December 7 victory over San Diego.

Bostic became the starting center and continued to handle the long-snapping duties the following season under new head coach Joe Gibbs, who had been the offensive coordinator of the Chargers. "He did what many new coaches do," Bostic said. "He came in and really cleaned house. A lot of the remnants of the 1980 team, from the Over-the-Hill-Gang, guys from the George Allen era, he got rid of a lot of them. He tried to implement that 'Air Coryell' offense [that had been successful for San Diego]. And after five games, we were 0–5, and I think he realized that he needed to fit the offense to the personnel. Instead of throwing the ball 55 times a game, we started running it 55 times a game.

"What I think the key was, after starting 0–5, was the ability to finish 8–8. We won eight of our last 11 games with basically four rookie linemen. I had never started. Melvin Jones had never started. [Joe] Jacoby, [Mark] May, and [Russ] Grimm had never started. George Starke was the only one that had any playing experience. I don't know if it's an NFL record, but I don't think any team has ever started the season with four offensive linemen who never had a career start."

That proved to just be the beginning of an outstanding 14-year career for Bostic with the Redskins. He would start in four Super Bowls, help earn three Lombardi Trophies, and be chosen to play in the Pro Bowl following the 1983 season, before retiring after the 1993 campaign.

Two Impressive Joes

From running back George Rogers, who was chosen first overall by New Orleans, to Phil Nelson, a tight end from Delaware, who was picked 332nd by Oakland, the NFL held its two-day draft in 1981 without Louisville's 6'7", 310-pound offensive tackle Joe Jacoby's name being announced.

But being a free agent was fine with Jacoby because it offered the opportunity to sign a contract with any team. And while several teams were interested, he agreed to a deal with the Redskins mainly for one reason: "[Offensive line coach] Joe Bugel. He's the one that stayed in contact with me through the whole process when the season was over and the scouting aspect of it went on late into the winter and spring," Jacoby said. "He just stayed involved with it, stayed on top of it. My mindset coming in, being a free agent and being one of anywhere from 115 to 125 guys in camp, was just to do my best, give it a shot, and see what happens. I guess I did catch their eye because of my ability with my quickness. Not quickness in my feet, but my athletic ability to play on the offensive line."

Once he was put through training camp drills and scrimmages while competing with seven veterans and five draft choices, some other examples of Jacoby's abilities surfaced: his work ethic, consistency, and his versatility.

"Yeah, I think that helped," said Jacoby, who was tried out at every position on the offensive line but center. "It helped during camp and being plugged in when you're in practice. All of a sudden they'd say, 'All right, go to left tackle.' Then you'd come out, and the next time they put you in at right guard. So [it was] being able to decipher the plays being called and basically it was knowing your right from your left and not making mistakes."

After alternating between guard and tackle for the first eight weeks, Jacoby was anchored down at left tackle, where he'd become a mainstay and a four-time Pro Bowler.

"Head Hog"

What began as a run-of-the-mill, coach-calling-his-players-a-name-during-training-camp-type incident in 1982, turned into a nickname-that-caught-the-attention-of-the-media-and-fans-alike-type deal.

"It started out as just a goof. We were just picking on [offensive line coach Joe] Bugel because training camp is kind of slow," said veteran tackle George Starke. "So we were just playing around and started wearing Hogs shirts.

"We recognized that training camp is boring for players, but it's even more boring for the media. So guys saw the Hogs shirts and were going, 'What's that about?' So then it kind of took on a life of its own and caught the attention of Washington's fans."

The original Hogs—Russ Grimm, Jeff Bostic, Mark May, Joe Jacoby, Don Warren, Rick "Doc" Walker, and Starke—garnered even more attention after the Redskins won eight of nine games during the

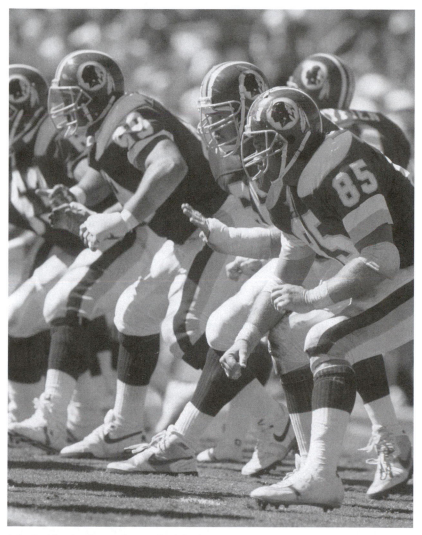

The Redskins' offensive line, colorfully known as "the Hogs," cleared the way to three Super Bowl titles during the first Joe Gibbs era. Photo courtesy of Getty Images

strike-shortened season behind the holes they were making in opposing defensive lines for running back John Riggins, who would become an honorary Hog. It continued during the victorious playoff run when Riggins carried the ball 37 times for 185 yards against Minnesota, and

36 times for 140 yards against Dallas. Washington's fans could have been described as being "Hog wild" by the time the team was preparing for Super Bowl XVII against Miami, which was being played in Southern California at the Rose Bowl.

"As we sort of barnstormed through the playoffs, going to L.A.— and I used to live in L.A. in the off-season—they're not excited about anything," Starke said. "They don't care about stars. They don't care about nicknames. They don't care about football. But the Hogs thing caught on in L.A.

"I was driving through Beverly Hills, and there were bed sheets on some mansions that said, 'GO HOGS!' It was the most bizarre thing. The Hogs phenomenon caught on in L.A. even.

"Timing is everything. That offensive line was the best. Maybe ever! The combination of the offense that [head coach Joe] Gibbs was running, the run offense, which was only one play, really, John, and the way we blocked—that whole combo—probably before that and after that has not been duplicated. So to be the best at that time, we were excited about that. It was kind of fun. It wouldn't have mattered if we weren't that good."

But they were that good. During the Super Bowl, the Hogs continued to lead the way for Riggins when he carried the ball 38 times for 166 yards, as Washington claimed its first Lombardi Trophy.

R.C. Comes to D.C.

Like an experienced game hunter, the Redskins knew that it's always better to reload than to run out of ammunition. That's why in 1985, they traded receiver Charlie Brown to the Atlanta Falcons for the rights to three-time Pro Bowl guard R.C. Thielemann.

"I thought it was great. I was a free agent. I wasn't in training camp. It was a money issue," said Thielemann, who had spent eight seasons with the Falcons. "In Atlanta, we had a couple good years, but at the time, Washington was in the middle of the [Joe] Gibbs years. It was a great offensive line, a great team, and a great opportunity for me to get a [Super Bowl] ring. I think that's what every kid dreams of."

With the acquisition of Thielemann, the Redskins strengthened their already potent offensive line by adding one more Hog to the barnyard, and he could not have been more pleased. "[The Hogs] were and probably will remain one of the premier units ever to play in the National Football League. You don't get a whole line that stays intact for years at a time, and Washington did. Of course, there were a couple pieces that got interchanged, but the core group of [Russ] Grimm, [Jeff] Bostic, [Mark] May, and [Joe] Jacoby were there as fixtures for years. And they were great guys. They all didn't run 4.5[-second] 40s and they all didn't look good in the showers, believe me, but they knew how to play football on Sunday."

Thielemann's first Sunday as one of Washington's first-stringers on September 29 against the Bears was unlike anything he had ever experienced as a Falcon. "I had never hurt my knee playing eight years of NFL football, and my first start with the Redskins was in Chicago on ol' Soldier Field, and I injured my knee," Thielemann said. "The ACL blew out on me. I missed the rest of that year and then came back, and the next year we went to the [1986 NFC] Championship Game and lost to the Giants. And the following year was the Super Bowl year."

Washington won 23 of 31 regular-season games during those two seasons following Thielemann's injury, as well as Super Bow XXII. He believes that the Redskins were successful because of their work ethic. And that admirable work ethic was a reflection of their head coach, Joe Gibbs.

"We had good players but I wouldn't say we were above and beyond anybody else in the league. We were just better prepared," said Thielemann. "I think with Gibbs, it's legendary that he probably never went home during the season. He just basically stayed at Redskin Park. And the other coaches, as well. There was just a total commitment during the season that they were not going to be outcoached."

Beating the Odds to Become a Hog

If nothing else, the Redskins learned right away that Raleigh McKenzie, an offensive lineman they had just chosen in the 11th round of the 1985 draft, was not a night owl. For that matter, neither was his twin brother, Reggie, a linebacker who was picked by the Raiders.

"It was a late call, like 1:00 in the morning," said McKenzie. "I thought the draft was over, but my brother had gotten a call about 12:00 or so. And, of course, he woke everybody up. His [selection] was in the 10th round, and I said, 'Well, they've got two more rounds. I may get a call.' And I fell back asleep."

Well rested when he reported to Washington's training camp, McKenzie knew that he had a limited time to make an impression on the coaches, and that that impression had better be good. "I was there for every practice and everything they were teaching me and telling me, I was doing everything they asked. So I think every time they threw me in there, there were no mental mistakes. I think I did really well. They had the rookie camp first, so we did our deal for a whole week. And then as soon as the veterans came in, you just kind of get on the backburner.

"[But guard] Ken Huff had to stay home for the first couple days, and so [offensive line coach] Joe Bugel stuck me in there early. I guess to see what I was made of. I think I impressed them right off the bat because I had to go up against [6'8", 320-pound veteran defensive tackle] Dave Butz."

Bugel was not the only one who was curious about what McKenzie was made of. So were the veteran offensive linemen. "Russ [Grimm], [Jeff] Bostic, Mark May, and [Joe] Jacoby—they kind of treated me like the rookie that I was. There wasn't too much love there," laughed McKenzie. "But I think once they saw me practice and things like that, they all took turns and gave me pointers here and there and kind of helped me along. So that was a good thing."

McKenzie deposited those pointers in his memory bank and performed well during camp and the preseason. That helped him to start gaining some confidence. "Once I started watching film, especially of other teams, the first thing that was in my mind was I thought I had the ability to play in this league. I just wanted that chance. Once the preseason games started, that's when they let the young guys play. If you understand what's going on and you know the plays and stuff, I got in there and did all that."

McKenzie did enough to beat the enormous odds and make the Redskins. And in his first start the following season on September 21 in San Diego, he was named as the Offensive Player of the Game.

What Time Is It? It's Simmons Time!

Ed Simmons doesn't have to be reminded that timing is everything—or what it means to be in the right place at the right time, regardless of the outcome.

It began when the offensive tackle was drafted by Washington in the sixth round of the 1987 draft out of Eastern Washington. "You wait around all day for the draft, and towards the end of the day you get picked up, and it's a relief. I was thinking it'd happen in an earlier round," Simmons said. "I thought around the fourth round, but when I got a call from the Redskins, it made everything okay. I felt great."

After reporting to training camp, the cross-country move and the adjustments Simmons had to face while making the jump from Division I-AA to the NFL were a little easier because of the Pacific Northwest roots he shared with a pair of teammates. "I had a couple of veterans show me different ropes," he said. "There were some guys that kind of welcomed you and made you feel like you're home. The two that stand out are [tight end] Clint Didier and [quarterback] Mark Rypien, being from the same area. I remember them…coming up to me with open arms and saying, 'Do you need a ride to the different facilities?' [That was] instead of riding the bus with the rest of the rookies.

"And I looked up to guys like [veteran offensive linemen] Mark May and Joe Jacoby. Those two guys, to me, they had it together. You want to look for a model to base yourself off of."

The roll call of rookies that head coach Joe Gibbs had started in season openers would likely take less time than for a Redskins fan to list what they admire about the Dallas Cowboys. Nevertheless, when Washington hosted the Philadelphia Eagles in the first game of the 1987 campaign on September 13, Simmons was in the starting lineup. His initial vision of what playing in the NFL was actually like stood across the line of scrimmage and looked a lot like All-Pro defensive end Reggie White.

He did fine against White and would make two more starts before suffering a season-ending injury on November 15 during a game against the Detroit Lions. "I injured my right knee going up against [312-pound defensive tackle] Jerry Ball. We got tangled up, and he landed on top of me," laughed Simmons. "My leg was behind me, and my knee gave."

By undergoing an operation and being placed on injured reserve, Simmons was a spectator when his teammates beat Denver in Super Bowl XXII. "I didn't really get to experience the full blow of it, but it was great. It was unbelievable that it was happening, that the team that I helped get there was at the top! But getting straight there in my rookie year, I didn't really experience the downside, what it takes to get there. I already knew what it took because we did it."

Keeping an unfortunate track record intact, while the Redskins were en route to their next Super Bowl in 1991, Simmons missed several games because of another knee injury. "I came back with four games left in the season," Simmons said. "I played sparingly in those four games and the two playoff games and then suited up for the Super Bowl [XXVI against Buffalo]. I only played, like, the last down, but just to get in the game.... But I was prepared and everything and pretty much experienced everything. The media day was pretty awesome. You see all the guys from ESPN and all the different newspapers and television affiliates. So that was a good deal."

Even with the knee injuries and subsequent surgeries, Simmons played in 142 games for Washington over 11 seasons before being released following the 1997 campaign in a salary cap move. Five years later, in 2002, he was named to the 70 Greatest Redskins Team.

"An Offensive Line Mercenary"

It would have been understandable if Jim Lachey had complained of dizziness when he landed in Washington in 1988.

Just before training camp opened that year, San Diego traded the fourth-year left offensive tackle up the coast to the then–Los Angeles Raiders. But after only one game, their season opener against, ironically, the Chargers, the Raiders jettisoned Lachey to the Redskins. Three teams in six weeks.

"I kind of found out early [the morning after the season opener] that a trade was going to go through for [quarterback] Jay Schroeder," said Lachey. "The Redskins opened on Monday night against the Giants. I remember watching that game and thinking, 'They didn't play Schroeder. It looks like I'm getting traded there tomorrow.' And so I went back to the hotel room and decided I should put my stuff together. I was basically living out of a suitcase for the six weeks that I was in training camp and then the opener. So I never really unpacked. I was kind of an offensive line mercenary that year."

A Pro Bowler the previous season, Lachey admits that his mind began to wander during the flight to Washington. He was uncertain of what was happening with his young career. "I was looking over all the things in the paper about [the Redskins-Giants] game and looking at their starting lineup, thinking, 'Here I go from being an All-Pro in the AFC to not even being a starter with the Redskins. Where was I going to fit in?' [Joe] Jacoby's been at left tackle forever. At the time, Mark May was in there at right tackle. R.C. Thielemann was at right guard, Russ Grimm and Raleigh McKenzie were [sharing time] at left guard, and Jeff Bostic was at center.

"I was thinking, 'Where am I going to play?' And so they ended up putting me at right tackle. That's kind of a big switch when you're used to playing left. But I was able to do that for five or six weeks and then they moved me towards the end of the season over to left tackle, and that's where I stayed," he recalled.

In addition to becoming acclimated to the position change, Lachey was also getting used to the fanatical atmosphere at RFK Stadium and around Washington in general. "I played at Ohio State, where we had 96,000 every week, screaming, nuts, crazy! I go to San Diego and it's such a transient area because of the military [bases] that most of the people that live there are from someplace else," Lachey said. "So if you're standing outside the stadium and we're playing the Steelers, if somebody scores, you don't know who it's for. I'm thinking, 'Man, this pro football is really different.'

"Then I go to RFK, and it was, 'No, it's not! This is what it's all about!' I don't know if it's the East Coast–West Coast mentality or what. I think it's just the fans in Washington. They knew the game, they knew the players, and they knew how to dissect a counter-trey better than Joe Bugel! It was amazing.

"You'd go to a store and they're telling you, 'You've got to pull this way. You're stepping with the wrong foot and you've got to use your hands more.' In San Diego, you'd go in there and it'd be, 'Dude. Why you so big?'"

Keeping His Mouth Shut and Eyes Wide Open

When guard Mark Schlereth reported to the Redskins training camp for the first time in 1989 after being drafted in the 10th round out of Idaho, he was, in essence, stepping into and sharing a locker room with history.

Four of Washington's offensive linemen: Russ Grimm, Joe Jacoby, Mark May, and Jeff Bostic, were entering their ninth season together as teammates. Founding members of the Hogs, they had played in three Super Bowls, winning two, and collectively had been chosen to play in 10 Pro Bowls. In short, they would have not only been able to sit at the "cool kids table," they could have done so while reclining on barcaloungers.

"I would have been excited to get drafted by the blind sisters of the poor," laughed Schlereth, the only offensive lineman drafted by Washington that year. "[But] I was very excited to get drafted by the Redskins because I knew they had had success."

In this case, was that success intimidating? "Of course there was pressure. I came in, in an era where I felt you didn't open your mouth unless you were spoken to. Unless you were asked a question, you basically kept your nose clean and did whatever the team was asking you to do and do it to the best of your ability. I didn't try to jump in and be one of the guys. I just kept to myself and went about my business and tried to earn the older veterans' respect."

Their respect began to come Schlereth's way after they witnessed his work ethic during camp and the early preseason games. "It was kind of a warming up process. I really don't have an exact moment [when I felt they had accepted me]," Schlereth said. "I just knew that even if they don't like me, they respected me because I went out and played hard and practiced hard. And that's really all I wanted, was [for] them to respect the fact that I was going to go out there and get the job done. And I suppose where I really felt accepted is when I started my first [regular-season] game [on November 12] against Philadelphia.

"Jeff Bostic and Russ Grimm took me under their wings. And Joe Jacoby did as well. We watched film together, and they showed me what to look for. So then, all of a sudden, I was part of the group."

Certainly a full-fledged member of the Hogs by his third season in 1991 when Washington captured the Super Bowl XXVI crown, Schlereth also became a Pro Bowler.

"That was exciting. That's a whole different deal. That's more about your individual accomplishments where the Super Bowl is just about being a team," said Schlereth, who would also be selected to play in the Pro Bowl in 1999 as a member of the Denver Broncos. "It was fun to go over [to Hawaii]. It was fun to represent the Redskins. And it was fun to have my family over there watching. It was definitely a nice treat. But once it's over, you realize how fleeting the moment is because you've got to go out and re-prove yourself every time you play."

Go Until You Can't

Akin to the lottery's catchphrase—you've got to be in it to win it!—in football, if you're not on the field, you're not in the game. Some players have a play-at-all-cost mentality. Jim Lachey was one of them.

During a playoff-game victory in Minnesota on January 2, 1993, the offensive tackle suffered a torn rib cartilage and had to receive pain-killing injections in order to stay on the field.

And even though he was unable to sleep much or practice at all the following week as the Redskins prepared for their next game in San Francisco, Lachey insisted on playing against the 49ers. The price? Ten more shots on game day. He played until team doctors and coaches forced him to stay on the sideline.

"That's what they're paying you to do. If there's a chance you can get on the field, you've got to give them that chance. Give yourself that chance," said Lachey. "I had a basketball coach in high school, and once I said I was sick. He said, 'Come in and get a good sweat and you'll feel better.' So I guess that's been my theory. Just go out there and go until you can't go anymore. And when they tell you that you can't go, that's when you shut it down. Some guys have higher thresholds for pain. Who knows?

"Ten injections into the ribs, I've got a knot there still. But that's what you do for the game. You go out there and have fun. We had a lot of guys that put themselves behind the team. The team's first! If I can help this team, I'm going to try to help the team. You want to do it for a guy like Coach Gibbs, to be honest with you. There was never any question. You just did it."

The following year, Lachey didn't have a choice. He tore the ACL and MCL in his right knee during the preseason opener against Cleveland and was out for the entire season. And in 1995 his rotator cuff, which had been hit countless times since he first donned shoulder pads and a helmet, finally went kaput.

"I got to a point where I couldn't even pull a belt on with my right arm. I couldn't touch my head to shampoo it," Lachey said. "You're getting in a stance and you've got that thing strapped up to you, and it just went. I knew it went! I knew there was nothing left. I'd put a lot of torque on that arm, so I knew sooner or later that it was going to go. I'm just happy it happened in my 11th year [and not sooner]. The doctor that looked at me said that it tore in stages because the tissue was different colors in different areas."

Missing 32 of 48 games during his final three seasons with the Redskins, the injuries and subsequent surgeries took their toll and sent Lachey into retirement prior to the 1996 campaign. "I think after having the knee surgery and then the [cleat-induced] gash on the calf and then my shoulder finally going out for the last time, I'm thinking, 'You know, this is enough. It's time to move on.' I had a lot of fun. I never kind of wanted to be a guy who just hung around to collect a paycheck. Football was a means to an end. I used it to get my education [from Ohio State University] and I used it to make money, and now I'm using that money to make more money."

chapter 9

Fondest Memories

"I liked Washington, period. It was a good city, a good football town. And the fans backed the team 100 percent. They did a lot of things for you. It was just a great town to be playing ball in."

—Coy Bacon, defensive end

•

"There are a lot of fond memories that I have, but I think more important are the relationships that I had with a number of players. I was very close to Brig Owens. Pat Fischer and I were very close. Chris Hanburger, Kenny Houston. These are players who were tremendous players in their own right. And to be associated with players like that, real pros, made me feel like, 'Mike, maybe you belong in this kind of company.'

"Keep in mind: I'm coming from being cut three times, once by the Packers and twice by the Lions. That said you aren't good enough. But after being with Washington and being exposed to these real, true professionals, it kind of changed my whole attitude. My confidence was built up. I felt like I had made some tremendous strides all because of the relationships that I had with these guys. I couldn't find a better group of professionals who prided themselves in their performance. I don't think I could find them anywhere, and I've been out of the game for 30 years and I have yet to find those types of people in the 'civilian life.'"

—Mike Bass, cornerback

•

"My [fondest memory is from my] rookie year [in 1957] when I was third in [the NFL] in rushing behind Jimmy Brown and Rick Casares. I broke one in the last game for 35, 40 yards, which would have put me very close to Jimmy, but it was called back because we had somebody offside. But just being up in that category with some great running backs made me feel real good. And, of course, playing in the [1960] Pro Bowl. Everybody likes to get there sooner or later, at least one time. And I was fortunate enough to do that."

—Don Bosseler, running back

•

"I guess for me it was the locker room and the guys, just the camaraderie. I had a lot of fun and can't single out any big thing. I was fortunate to play with [Charles] Mann and [Dexter] Manley, [Neal] Olkewicz, [Alvin] Walton, [Darrell] Green, all those guys.

"My most memorable moment probably was when [Giants tight end] Mark Bavaro caught a touchdown on me my rookie year and my head was face down in the dirt. It ended up in *Sports Illustrated*, and I bought about 30 copies. I was so happy I made it in the magazine even though it was in a bad light. I had to laugh at it."

—Todd Bowles, safety

•

"The most memorable moment I had in a game was when I gained 191 yards against the Giants in New York [on October 29, 1972]. Just getting 100 yards is tough, but getting almost 200 yards is remarkable. I don't remember every carry, but I remember some of the fans there didn't particularly like my performance. Someone threw a big can of beer at me in the end zone, and it wasn't even my brand.

"[Having played for the Redskins] is almost like having a hobby that happened to be something that you were extremely good at. That you were able to do so well that people even today come up to me and congratulate me or tell me what a great player I was then. It's no different than being an excellent chess player, however, in a different venue."

—Larry Brown, running back

•

"We were playing the Cowboys in 1972 for the NFC championship. It was in the fourth quarter, and we'd just kicked a field goal to go ahead 20–3. Jon Jaqua tackled the kickoff guy for the Cowboys on, like, the 11-yard line, and the whole stands were going, 'Defense! Defense!'—and stomping their feet. You know how RFK Stadium got. It was so loud that I was in the huddle and Jack Pardee was calling the play. My helmet was only about a foot and a half away from his, and I couldn't hear him. I couldn't hear a thing.

"The Cowboys broke the huddle and came up to the line of scrimmage, and they were just looking around like, 'What in the hell did we get ourselves into?' We stopped them one, two, three, and they had to punt. You almost couldn't stand up because the sound was so loud. It was just an incredible moment."

—Bill Brundige, defensive lineman

•

"There were very eventful years that I had with the Redskins. There were two strikes, two Super Bowls, and a whole list of injuries and everything else. But I wouldn't trade those experiences. I say that because, football in particular, but just athletics at the professional level is a microcosm of life in the sense that you go from being relatively unknown, to being an established veteran, to being out of the game. And in my case, it took place over a six-year period.

"It's basically what we're going to see in our business careers. We're going to see us establishing a base, working hard, getting our name out there and becoming respected by our peers, hopefully. I feel a lot better prepared now for facing what I am facing because of what I've been through in professional athletics."

—Ken Coffey, safety

•

"My fondest memory, I guess, was Richie Petitbon's year as head coach [in 1993] and the Atlanta Falcons game we had [on December 19] at

RFK [which the Redskins won, 30–17]. I think I had two or three sacks, a forced fumble, an interception, and a fumble recovery for a touchdown. It was just a real good day for me."

—Monte Coleman, linebacker

•

"I remember being a rookie and being around so many great players and just the whole aura and mystique of Redskin Park, the Hogs, and just being there with Joe Gibbs in those years. It just really felt like it was a privilege for a young player to be a part of something so wonderful in sports history, not just Redskins history. That was one of the most amazing times for any franchise in all of sports history. I was just so grateful to be a part of it."

—Andre Collins, linebacker

•

"We had a nucleus of guys that knew how to win games and we went out and did it. Besides Theismann and Riggins and Dave Butz, we had a lot like myself, a 12th-rounder on a wing and a prayer to make the team. And not to say that we didn't have the ability, because we did, to win three Super Bowls. I looked at us as a bunch of blue-collar workers that went out and got the job done."

—Clint Didier, tight end

•

"A lot of players were telling me when we played the Giants [in the Meadowlands] the first time in my rookie year [on October 27, 1991], 'We haven't beaten the Giants in six straight times. So let's do our jobs.' I said, 'Hey, I wasn't here in those six straight times. So I'm just going to go out there and play like I know how.' And when Coach Gibbs put me in after halftime, for me to get 80 yards and provide a spark for the team [to win, 17–13]—that was one of my fondest memories."

—Ricky Ervins, running back

•

"My fondest memory was the day I went out to practice [as a rookie in 1972] and was recognized as a member of the team. After that first training camp, they said, 'You need to go find yourself an apartment because you're going to be a part of the team.' That was an exciting day for me."

—Frank Grant, running back

.

"It was the first year [1994], and it...[was] more the people that were around—Monte Coleman, Tim Johnson, and the guys around me—that really made it fun. To give you an exact thing, I don't have necessarily an exact thing. I just remember me and Monte Coleman working out together. For me, he looked like the ultimate linebacker, had the look of a linebacker, the attitude of a linebacker. We just really pushed each other in the weight room. And then Tim Johnson would have me go through drills to try to get me better as a pass rusher. And then outside of that, they actually spoke into my life, just as a person, as a man. So it was really a good time.

"What I'm most proud of is at the end of the day when fans come up and say that we appreciated your game because you played hard all the time. That to me, obviously I enjoyed the sacks, but when someone says that they appreciate that you gave your all, and when you know and felt like you gave your all, it's good to get that type of recognition."

—Ken Harvey, linebacker

.

"The Monday night game [October 8, 1973] against the Dallas Cowboys when I stopped Walt Garrison [on fourth down with 10 seconds left in the game] somewhere very close to the goal line [to preserve a 14–7 victory and move both teams into a tie atop the NFC East]—that has probably remained with me more than anything else throughout my retirement.

"But we had a lot of good times there. I think that the things that can't be measured or people don't know about is the camaraderie among the players. That was a very, very good group of guys to play with. They were experienced ballplayers and they knew where they were headed in terms of life. When you look back on it and see a group like that, most of those guys have been pretty successful in their own way after football."

—Ken Houston, safety

•

"The consistency of winning. I had been in Pittsburgh for five years and we never won anything. I experienced great individual success, but no team success. I go to Baltimore [in 1970] and we win the Super Bowl [V], and now I'm hoping that type of success continues. And basically to a degree, it did continue in Washington. So my fondest memory is basically that fans across the country and all the teams across the country knew that we were a good football team. And that if you came to play us, you had to have it together or you're going to lose."

—Roy Jefferson, receiver

•

"My fondest memory was 1969 and having the opportunity to play under Vince Lombardi. That was the highlight of 18 years [in the NFL]. By far! We had a big year offensively that year.

"People don't realize what a sense of humor he had. He had great leadership qualities and he was so fun. I mean, he was fun to be around. And I really enjoyed his method of coaching. You worked. Everybody worked. There was no wasted time on the field. You practiced an hour and a half and you got off, instead of two hours where you wasted 45 minutes standing around watching something. Everybody participated. He was by far the most organized and best football coach. And that was the highlight for me.

"And having talked, before he even came to the Redskins, with [Green Bay's] Bart Starr and Paul Hornung and Max McGee, people that had played for him, they said, 'You will love him.' And I did. I understood why they had had great success."

—Sonny Jurgensen, quarterback

•

"My fondest memory is just the association with the guys that I played with. Every one of them were winning guys. I was on teams for 10 years that were losers, especially in New Orleans. [With the Redskins] it was fun to go to practice every day, fun to go to meetings. We had a lot of laughs. For the first three years there, we had team parties every Tuesday night and most everybody showed up for them.

"I guess going to the Super Bowl in 1972 would be a highlight. But also, we won a lot of games there in seven years with George Allen. I think we won more games in a seven-year period than any team in the NFL."

—Billy Kilmer, quarterback

•

"The people. I played on teams with great people. They're still very close friends of mine. Also, the Redskins fans were very good fans to play for. So those are two great memories that I'll always cherish."

—Paul Krause, safety

•

"One of my fondest memories…I think just the camaraderie we had as a football team. We'd be in practice and sometimes we would turn it up. Man, we had great practices. See, I believed you practice the way you're going to play. We had physical practices.

"My fondest memory, I have to tell you, is just going up against [offensive tackle] Joe Jacoby. We had everybody on offense and defense just watching us go one-on-one with each other. We're out there battling it out. And it was great. It was just fantastic to be a part of it. Just being a part of a group that sort of embraced [it]. We all had the same common denominator and that was to win, and to work hard, and to embrace our coaches."

—Dexter Manley, defensive end

•

"I have several. Practicing in the freezing cold, the offense would go last and the defense would go first. Meaning the first-team defense would go against the scout-team offense and then it would switch, and the scout-team defense would go against the first-team offense. And Art Monk, Gary Clark, and a bunch of those guys, since they weren't going yet, would sneak in and wait inside and stay warm. The defensive guys couldn't get away with it. Our coaches wouldn't let us. But laughing at Art Monk sticking his head out the door to see if it was time for the offense to go, that's kind of a funny memory.

"And then there's Dexter [Manley] getting injured one day. He really wasn't injured; he just got hurt a little bit. But it wasn't as dramatic as he made it. He was lying on the ground, crawling, and telling Perry Brooks and I to go get the guy that hurt him. He was like, 'Charles! Get that guyyyy!' Very dramatic. He could have probably won an Emmy or an Oscar for that role."

—Charles Mann, defensive end

•

"It was the guys, a bunch of class guys. Once you win a Super Bowl with a group of guys, you have that bond forever. We had a bunch of guys with good character, hard workers, guys who were dedicated to the organization. When you look at the guys in that locker room when I came there in '89, they were just guys that you wanted to model yourself after as a player in the NFL—Doug Williams, Charles Mann, Darrell Green, Russ Grimm, Mark Rypien, Art Monk, Monte Coleman, guys of that caliber. I think that was special, the way that team was put together and the quality of players that we had."

—Martin Mayhew, cornerback

•

"Just being a Redskin at that time. Playing for Joe Gibbs and Bobby Beathard and Mr. Cooke was an experience. And I think the camaraderie with the players is the thing that I remember the most.

"And playing for Richie Petitbon! He doesn't get the credit that he really deserves as a defensive coordinator. I think Richie was the greatest adjuster in the history of that league. He was fantastic. One of the best minds that I've ever seen and been around and played against. He's great. I love Richie."

—LeCharls McDaniel, cornerback

•

"Going to Super Bowl [VII] even though we lost was exciting. And the relationship we had with the guys because we'd all been somewhere and done something ourselves. We'd all been All-Pros or something. But here we are, thirty-something years old and over, and we were still having success playing against a bunch of kids."

—Ron McDole, defensive end

•

"Frankly, the people. I grew up in Los Angeles, I played at the Coliseum parts of three decades because I went to 'SC and I went to high school down the street. I always liked the Los Angeles fans, but the enthusiasm from the Washington fans was second to none. They were wonderful people. They were certainly aware of two things: politics and pro football. And I'm not sure that pro football wasn't higher than politics with most of the people."

—Marlin McKeever, linebacker

•

"There's no doubt about it, the fondest memory of a game that I have is when we played Dallas before the first Super Bowl [in the NFC Championship Game on January 22, 1983]. The crowd at [RFK Stadium] was going crazy, and Dexter [Manley] hit [Cowboys quarterback Gary Hogeboom], and Darryl Grant intercepted the ball and went in for a touchdown. For some reason, the Super Bowls are secondary to most of the Cowboys games.

"It was a great rivalry. At that time, we were both playing pretty well, and it seemed like every game you were actually playing for something. And then the Giants games became that type of thing also."

—Rich Milot, linebacker

•

"Winning the Super Bowl [XXVI] is probably the best that I ever remember. But as I think back to the Redskin days, after we won the Super Bowl we had some trying years. I tried to play my butt off, and one thing that I remember is the fans. When you're out there playing and you lose a game, you sometimes wonder—do people still see what you're doing? And I think a lot of fans and a lot of people around here recognized that I was still trying to give my best. Whether we win, lose, or draw, I was going to give you everything I had. That made me feel good that they really paid that close of attention."

—Brian Mitchell, running back

•

"I was there when we opened D.C. Stadium [on October 1, 1961, against the New York Giants]. The first year I played [in 1960], we were in the old Griffith Stadium. And I remember, it might have been one of the last games we played, there was kind of a unique memory in that it started snowing about 10:00 in the morning. The snow was really heavy and wet, and it snowed so fast that they couldn't get the tarp up off the field. So they just had to leave it down. We played the Giants [on December 11] and were ahead of them, I believe, 3–0 late in the game. Mike Nixon was the coach and he told the punt returner to just let the ball go, to not field it, and hopefully we could run out the clock. But for some reason, this guy decided to field the ball and he fumbled it. They got the ball at our 5-yard line and scored.

"At that point, I thought this coaching business is pretty rough. When you tell a guy that's been around a while what to do and then he doesn't do it and you lose the game—I think two or three weeks later, they fired Mike Nixon, and Bill McPeak came in and took over."

—Tom Osborne, receiver

•

"[In the 1968 season opener in Chicago on September 15, it was my sixth season in the NFL, and] I think that really showed what [quarterback] Sonny [Jurgensen] could do. My father passed away while I was in college, and that was the only game my mother had really seen. She and some of my family came down [from Madison, Wisconsin], and he just made it happen. He just said, 'Get open and we'll get it to you.' And he did! I had [a career-high] three touchdowns that day [in the 38–28 victory]. That to me, in my mind, stands out. He knew about my family and whatever and just made it happen.

"[Aside from that Bears game] I would say the games against Dallas [are fond memories]. They were always a treat whether in Washington or in Dallas. My recollection is going into Dallas several times and just marveling at some of the games that Sonny would have. He didn't tell a lot of people, but his arm hurt him badly. A lot of times, he'd go into the huddle and just kind of tell everybody to take off and he'd throw it as far and as hard as he could and make everybody think he could throw long from that point on.

"He'd be moaning and would just hold his arm because it really was hurting him. But he gave the Cowboys the impression that he could go long if he had to. But really, in the back of his mind, it was probably not going to happen. But he made them think it, anyway."

—Pat Richter, tight end/punter

•

"I played with a group of guys that had the same demeanor, the same outlook. It was kind of like there weren't really a lot of superstars outside of Art Monk. I think it was a group of guys that came to work every day with a lunchbox and went at it and sold themselves in whatever capacity.

"I remember some of the practices on Wednesdays were probably more intense than some of our games on Sundays. I think that one of Joe Gibbs' trademarks is the fact that he believed in that. As players, we always wanted to say, 'Joe, if there's one thing, loosen up a little bit on Wednesdays and Thursdays.' And every time he did, we'd end up blowing it on Sundays. We'd lose a game.

"He believed in a way. I think we all kind of believed in it. There was a period of time there when we weren't even looking forward to the next time we got a crumb thrown to us because most of the time it backfired."

—Mark Rypien, quarterback

•

"Every year you go to training camp, and it's, 'We've got to win the big game and we've got to win!' Never get there, never get there, and never get there, and finally in your 13th year [in the league you do].… So many guys don't get that opportunity. Not only to get there, but to win it.

"My twin brother [Rich] played 12 years with the Rams. They played the Steelers in the '79 season [Super Bowl XIV]. They almost beat them, but they didn't. So he's got a runner-up ring. I have the real deal."

—Ron Saul, guard

•

"Obviously, winning Super Bowl [XXVI] is a fond memory, but it's more about the relationships I had and still have to this day with a lot of guys that played on those teams that really cared for me as a person, not just as a football player. Guys like Monte Coleman, Art Monk, Charles Mann, and Darrell [Green]. So a lot of that is that those guys are my friends for life. And when I retired [in April 2001, after 12 seasons, the first six with the Redskins] guys like Joe Jacoby calling up and saying, 'Hey, congratulations.' That's great.

"It's guys that you might not talk to for a month or two or three or four at a time, but as soon as you bump into each other or as soon as you call one another, it's like you never spent a minute apart. Those relationships are special and they last a lifetime."

—Mark Schlereth, guard

•

"We played in the Hall of Fame Game in Canton, Ohio [on August 5, 1989, against Buffalo], and just going there and just being in the Hall of Fame and walking around and seeing all the greats. One day, I'm going to go back and visit that place again and really get the full effect because it really put everything in perspective. Just how far we've come in the NFL."

—Ed Simmons, tackle

•

"Playing with Sonny [Jurgensen], maybe. I knew at that time that there was something special about him. And so to be a kid and be in the huddle with Sonny was pretty special.

"I think football's a job like any other job. I'm proud of the fact that I worked pretty hard at it and I gave you a day's work for a day's pay. And I would like to say that we were all like that. We were always essentially a blue-collar, give-them-a-day's-work-for-a-day's-pay-type team. We were surrounded by a lot of really fine, fine people. To play with guys like Pat Fischer and Larry Brown and Sonny Jurgensen, up through "Riggo" and the Hogs, the Redskins have always tended to pick a certain type of person. The Redskins essentially picked good guys, but tough guys. It was nice to be around them."

—George Starke, tackle

.

"Certainly winning the championship was wonderful, but the most enjoyable game I ever played in as a Redskin was the NFC Championship Game here in front of our fans against the Dallas Cowboys in January of '83. I stood on the field at the end of the game, and the field was actually shaking because the people were pounding on the aluminum seats. It was unbelievable.

"But for me, the thing I'm most proud of is that I played in 163 consecutive football games. I never missed a day of work. I gave it everything I had from practice to playing."

—Joe Theismann, quarterback

.

"Every year it's winning football games. It's great! You got to play [NFC East rivals] Philadelphia twice, the Giants twice, and Dallas twice [a year]. And those were great teams. As an adult playing a game, it was fun. It was a great time, a great way to end a [12-year, four as a Redskin] career."

—R.C. Thielemann, guard

.

"I remember after the NFC Championship Game in '72, we beat Dallas, 26–3. Bob Brunet, who was another special-teams guy, we walked into the [popular Washington restaurant] Duke Zeibert's, and the people that were in there gave us a standing ovation. It was really incredible!"

—Rusty Tillman, linebacker

chapter 10

Stunts, Swim Moves, and Sacks

"I Was Scared to Death!"

Washington's top draft choice in 1970, Bill Brundige was the first defensive lineman the team had chosen with its first pick in nine years. And as if that wasn't enough pressure on him, take into account that he was chosen by Vince Lombardi, who had coached the Redskins for one season after a legendary tenure in Green Bay. The defensive end from Colorado was, let's just say, less than tranquil.

"I was scared to death! I had just read a book by Jerry Kramer called *Instant Replay*, and he chronicled what the practices were like with the Packers and what Lombardi was like," said Brundige. "About the only team in the NFL that had not contacted me prior to the draft were the Redskins. Then I got a phone call, and the secretary said, 'Bill Brundige, you have a call from Washington. Please hold the line.' I'm thinking, 'I don't know anybody in Seattle or Tacoma.' Then [Lombardi] came on the line, and I about dropped the phone. I was in a state of shock!"

Brundige may have been much calmer when he arrived for minicamp, but that doesn't mean that he didn't have a lot on his mind. And it had nothing to do with football or Lombardi.

"That was during the height of the Vietnam War, so I went down to the draft board and said, 'I'm going to be playing for the Washington Redskins. I don't really want to go to Vietnam, show me some of the parameters.' So the draft board gave me a book and says, 'Here are things that we can't take.' I looked, and it had a height and weight chart. And if I weighed over 270, then I would be ineligible. So I started eating!"

After having gained enough weight to overtip the scales for the service, Brundige's extra poundage didn't go over too well with Lombardi.

"We sat down in his office, and he says, 'What do you weigh now?' I said, 'Oh, about 275.' That was 25 pounds more than I weighed two months before," Brundige said. "He just looked at me, shook his head, and said, 'I think it would be a good idea for you to report to camp as close to your college playing weight as possible.'

"I tried like heck, but I couldn't lose the weight. The third day of camp, I was walking up a hill and talking with Mike McCormack, the defensive line coach, and Coach Lombardi is at the top of the hill. He says, 'Hey, Bill! What did you weigh in at?' I couldn't lie. I said, 'Um, uh, uh 272.' And he had that Cheshire grin and those dark glasses and he just looked at me, grinned, and just shook his head a little bit and walked away. My knees were shaking. I mean, literally shaking! He was one of the most intimidating people I've ever met."

Brundige never had an opportunity to play a game for the coaching legend. Lombardi passed away on September 3, 1970, 17 days before the season opener.

The Over-the-Hill Gang Kid

Other than maybe gymnastics, in what sport can someone in their mid-twenties be considered over the hill? Certainly not football.

However, when Diron Talbert came to Washington in 1971 with his Los Angeles Rams coach of four years, George Allen, the defensive tackle would soon be grouped with the older veterans whom Allen had acquired and be a part of the Over-the-Hill Gang.

"George had brought in Pat Fischer, Ron McDole, Billy Kilmer, Maxie Baughan, Boyd Dowler, and then me," said Talbert. "I was 27 and they were all 32, 33, or 34. But I was proud to be there. I wanted to be a member of the Over-the-Hill Gang. I knew it was something that would probably go down in history as one of the oldest teams able to compete."

At 9–4–1, the oldsters, youngsters, and somewhere-in-betweensters posted Washington's most victories in 29 years and made the playoffs for the first time since 1945. Or, in other words, a year after Talbert was born. But they were just getting started. Because in 1972 the Redskins were an impressive 11–3, beat their division-rival Dallas Cowboys for the conference crown, and met Miami in Super Bowl VII.

"The most exciting thing was that we won the championship game, the first time Washington's won a championship in years. I got trapped and almost suffocated from the exhaustion of trying to get off the field with all the fans on the field [celebrating after we beat the Cowboys, 26–3]. Literally 10,000 to 15,000 were on the field," Talbert said. "The Super Bowl game was a lot of fun to be there and to do that. Losing it certainly was not a highlight. It was reality."

A Bear Dances into D.C.

One coach's aging veteran is another coach's player with invaluable experience. In this case, George Allen was the latter coach and defensive end Ron McDole was the player.

Acquired from the Bills on May 11, 1971, for future draft choices, McDole, a two-time AFL All-Star, was heading into his 11th season and saw the writing on the wall in Buffalo. He would become anxious to read what was scribbled on the walls in Washington.

"John Rauch was [the head coach in Buffalo] and was changing things. He was getting rid of people and trying to build his own team," said McDole. "It was obvious that he felt some of us older players wouldn't be available when he got his team together, I guess. Everybody kind of anticipated that something was going to happen. You're always kind of scared. You don't know what it's like going someplace else when you've been somewhere for quite a while.

"George called me up and, of course, he was a very enthusiastic individual. I think the first words were, 'Well, how's it feel to be with a winner?' He wanted me to come to [Washington] immediately to meet him. That kind of made you feel like you're welcome.

"And I knew some guys [who were with the Redskins]. Billy Kilmer and I started out together. And Pat Fischer and I went to college together and were captains at Nebraska. So there were people on the team that I knew very well. And then when I got there with the Over-the-Hill Gang, it was like old home week."

But at 32 and despite what his former coach may have felt, McDole, who would later be nicknamed "the Dancing Bear" by teammate Sonny Jurgensen, didn't feel over the hill. He felt the move to Washington was a breath of fresh air and renewed his enthusiasm for the game. As far as being labeled as one of the Over-the-Hill Gang, the veteran took it as a compliment.

"Basically at that time, when you got [to be] 30 and over, [teams] were trying to replace you. And George was picking people up," McDole said. "We used to celebrate people's birthdays when they became 30. It was a big deal.

"George was the type of guy who felt that the older guys made fewer mental mistakes and had more experience and knowledge. So he could do a lot more on the field. Especially on defense! He basically was a defensive coach. He felt if somebody lost a step or something like that, they'd make it up without making the mistakes."

A Big Self-Scouter

Washington's George Allen used a substitution to make an addition in 1975. Make that a huge addition. After having signed 6'7", 295-pound free agent defensive tackle Dave Butz, the NFL directed the Redskins to compensate St. Louis with their first-round draft choices in 1977 and 1978, and a second-round pick in 1979.

It was a heavy price, considering that Butz, who was going into his third season, sat out all but one game of the 1974 campaign because of a severe hamstring injury. "They gave up way too much," said Butz, who had a brief conversation that didn't go too well with the Cardinals after his contract expired. "Rick Sullivan, the personnel manager for the Cardinals said, 'We don't know what Dave Butz can do.' He sat not more than six inches from me and said, 'We don't think Dave can play in the NFL,' while we were trying to renegotiate my contract. That, from getting the firsts and a second, totally amazed me. It was shocking. I was appalled that they gave up so much, but once that's done, it's done. My

Defensive lineman Dave Butz won two Super Bowls during his 14 seasons with the Redskins. Photo courtesy of Getty Images

job was to play football. Fortunately, none of the players they got for me, not a one of them, helped [St. Louis] win a game."

Butz, on the other hand, would get a whole new education on how to prepare for and play the game. And he helped Washington right away. "I really learned quite a bit. It was a more complex defense from just lining up and going to one that had, I guess—[linebacker] Chris Hanburger knew at one time—150 different audibles. We had different types of line stunts and things of that nature which we never had with the Cardinals. And then there was also a lot of technique that you had to learn."

He would also get lessons away from the field and credits what he picked up in the film room for why he would go on to play in 203 games over 14 seasons for the Redskins and be credited with 59.5 sacks.

"I would critique myself as I would another player to see if I was tipping off or giving anything away that another team could use against me. That was very effective," Butz said. "Studying film was very important. By the time I played most teams, I would have watched five [of their] game films. I had a good idea of what was going to happen before they even came up to the line.

"A lot of players will talk to each other if they're going to do a block. The tackle will be set apart from the guard, and all of a sudden he's a little closer, and that set bells off. The tackle even sometimes had their feet placed down aiming at you, so I had to make [defensive end] Charles Mann aware, 'Hey! The play's going outside because he's going to block down on me.' They'll give it away on film. Some guards put their heel up on a pass and put their heel down on a run [once they're in a stance]. So there's a lot of little things that you can pick up prior to the snap of the ball."

Not a Fan of Crackback Blocks

Perry Brooks' NFL career didn't start off as well as he would have liked. Drafted and released by New England in 1976, the Redskins signed him the following season. However, during the second preseason game in Miami, the defensive tackle found out that a full speed collision with an offensive guard doesn't always end well.

"I was chasing good ol' [Dolphins quarterback] Bob Griese, and Bob Kuechenberg came and hit me with a crackback block, and I messed up some ligaments in my knee. I didn't tear anything, I just sprained it severely," said Brooks. "He broke two bones in his back on the play, so it was a very, very vicious hit. It was pretty dramatic. I was having a great game, too."

Placed on injured reserve, Brooks had the opportunity to learn about pro football from some of the veterans who had taken him under their wing. "Diron Talbert kind of showed me and taught me what it took to be a professional football player," he said. "I owe a lot to him and some other veterans, as well. Joe Lavender was a great friend and showed me the ropes. Coy Bacon happened to come in at that time, and we had Dave Butz, who was a quiet man and didn't say that much.

"Also at that time, Harold McLinton was the middle linebacker. He was a Southern University alumni, like myself, and he showed me the ropes, also. We had a lot of veterans that went out and tried to show the young players what it took to be successful in the National Football League."

After playing under head coach Jack Pardee for three seasons, Brooks made a career-high 12 starts in 1981 under Washington's rookie head coach Joe Gibbs. Unfortunately, he was sidelined again during the strike-shortened 1982 season after breaking his fibula because of another crackback block in the team's only loss of the year on December 5 versus Dallas. "It was on the first play of the game. I didn't know it was broken, I just thought it was very bruised," Brooks said. "Then I came to find out it was broken. From there, it was downhill as far as not being a starter anymore and being a pass-rush specialist."

Broken leg or no broken leg, the defensive tackle turned pass-rush specialist was not going to miss playing in Super Bowl XVII. The Redskins earned the league title by beating Miami, 27–17. "They brought me back, and I did play in certain situations. It was just a bad-luck thing. I was having a good year up to the point we went on strike."

Brooks was healthy in 1983 for what would be his sixth of seven seasons with the Redskins and helped the club try to capture back-to-back titles. They, however, were crushed in Super Bowl XVIII by the Raiders, 38–9. "I just think it wasn't our day," said Brooks. "Unfortunately, some things happened against us in that particular game."

Making Believers His Whole Career

Coy Bacon was certainly experienced but far from over the hill when Cincinnati traded him to the Redskins along with cornerback Lemar Parrish on draft day in 1978. The three-time Pro Bowl defensive end had joined the league in 1968 as a 26-year-old rookie and proceeded to play five seasons with the Los Angeles Rams, three seasons with San Diego, and two with the Bengals. He arrived in Washington as an acknowledged pass rusher, ready to keep working and well aware that the NFL is indeed a business.

"It was just about being traded again," Bacon said, matter-of-factly. "I had asked for more money because I had 26 sacks with Cincinnati in 1976. They didn't want to pay me because of my age and they thought maybe I was going downhill. So they traded me."

Fortunately for the Redskins, "going downhill" may not have been the most accurate prediction to come from the Bengals' brain trust. "My first year [in Washington]," Bacon said, "I had 15 sacks and was part of the leadership. The guys respected me, and I respected them. We had a good team, a veteran team. There weren't many rookies on the team, so we all played a role in different ways."

It seemed to Bacon that his role since his rookie season with the Rams was to continually prove that he belonged in the league. "People didn't think I'd make it at all," said Bacon, who was released after three games into his fourth season with the Redskins. "I wasn't a draft choice. I came out of a semi-pro league in Charleston, West Virginia. The Dallas Cowboys brought me out of that league, and I started playing in the NFL and kept going up, escalating on up to first-string [and eventually] 15 years in the NFL. A lot of people didn't count on me to make it far or that long, but I had confidence in myself. That and God-given talent kept me going."

"Like I'm Going to Lateral the Ball"

If a cornerback is often referred to as a receiver who can not catch too well, what is a defensive end who snares passes like a center fielder called? Try Ron McDole.

During his eight seasons with the Redskins (1971–1978) and 10 seasons before that with Buffalo, Houston, and St. Louis, the 6'4", 265-pounder recorded 12 interceptions off of the likes of star quarterbacks Roger Staubach, Joe Namath, and Bob Griese.

"You're playing against a guy over you who probably is just as good as you are. And if you can win 51 percent of the battles, you should have a big game," said McDole. "So you're fighting constantly to get to the passer, and all of a sudden you're free. If the guy didn't fall down or have a heart attack, then there's something up.

"I'd line up in my regular stance and then I would bail out and pick up a lot of screens. I think they threw to me because they were shocked to see 300 pounds trying to run backwards. Most of them were screens, and some of them I batted back up into the air when they tried to throw over me."

Of all the quarterbacks that McDole picked off, he recalls Namath as the only one who had something to say about what happened afterward. "He always backed out [at the snap], he didn't turn from the center," McDole said. "So he was backing out one way, and I was backing out the other way. And as I was backing out, I was excited and kind of lost my balance and started stumbling backwards, and he threw the ball right to me.

"After the game, I told him, 'I really appreciate your throwing me a pass.' And he said, 'I didn't throw it to you. I saw you falling backwards and I started laughing and I couldn't get it over your head.'"

On one other occasion, October 10, 1971, just his fourth game with the Redskins, McDole's receiving prowess resulted in a trip to the end zone. Not a speedy trip, mind you, but it still counted in Washington's 22–13 victory. "That was against [Oilers quarterback] Charley Johnson. He tried to throw a screen," said McDole, who collected three of his six career interceptions as a Redskin that season. "The funny thing about that is Verlon Biggs was playing the other [defensive] end and was coming across the field from the other side as we rushed the passer. I picked the screen off and started running, and Verlon started running up front blocking for me. Then he pulled in behind me, and he always called me Dole. He said, 'Lateral, Dole! You're not going to make it! Lateral! Lateral!'

"So I got into the end zone and he jumped on top of me and said, 'I didn't think you'd get here.' And I said, 'Well, I'd have got here sooner if you'd block somebody.' Like I'm going to lateral the ball. How many opportunities did I get to score?"

Mr. Versatility

At times when you watch a football game, it seems that one guy is involved in practically every play. At Rice University, Darryl Grant was that guy. He would line up at tackle or center on offense and at linebacker or nose guard on defense. He was also the long snapper on special teams. In a word, Grant was versatile. And that would serve him well after being drafted by the Redskins in 1981.

"The more you can do, the more you will do," said Grant, who was a ninth-round selection. "When they drafted me, I was a little bit nervous. I'm looking at the guys I'd been watching on TV and I knew this was the next level. This was the highest level. I just knew that I had to do the best I could. I had nothing to lose. Go out there and run as hard as I could, hit as hard as I could, and learn what to do and see where I stood."

After Grant made the team and spent his rookie year on special teams and as a backup offensive lineman, Washington's head coach Joe Gibbs thought that Grant should stand with the defensive linemen and switched him. "I saw it as an opportunity. I knew I could do it because in college, a lot of games, I was assigned to whoever the toughest guy was on the other team. Where the guy was lined up, that's where I would play," Grant said. "In my mind, football was football. Where I lined up didn't matter to me that much.

"I was hoping at one point they would give me a shot in the back-field when everybody was doing the big guy 'Refrigerator' thing. I was a prime candidate for that, I thought. But they chose not to do that at all."

And while it wasn't in the backfield behind Joe Theismann, Grant did see his first extended playing time on December 5, 1982, when the Redskins hosted Dallas and starting defensive tackle Perry Brooks suffered a broken leg. They were tagged by the Cowboys, 24–10, for their only loss during the strike-shortened season.

A Manley among Men

As colorful as Pablo Picasso's finest work and at times standing out like Vincent van Gogh's missing ear, Redskins defensive end Dexter Manley was a sack artist during the 1980s. Make that *the* sack artist.

Beginning in 1983, his third season in the NFL and first as a full-time starter, Manley recorded 11 sacks and began a four-year run of double-digit sack totals, including a team-record 18 in 1986. "The main thing was you always have to know your opponent, but most important, you had to have a desire to get to the quarterback," Manley said. "I knew

Dexter Manley won two Super Bowls during his nine seasons in Washington.

that, as a defensive end, most coaches always say that you have to play the run first and get to the quarterback. But I was more of an 'I' guy. So I wanted to really be something special, and I just knew principally I was built for speed and quickness, and I knew that's what I had.

"There was nobody getting off the football like me in those days. [Minnesota's] Chris Doleman and [the Raiders'] Howie Long would get off the football, but I felt like I had the edge over everybody. And really, the ingredient was our offense really put up a lot of points, and that allowed the defense to be more aggressive. And so because of that, I was able to utilize my abilities in being able to get to the quarterback."

With a team-record 97.5 sacks during his nine seasons in Washington, the two-time All-Pro feels that he did his job while frustrating opposing offensive tackles and coaches alike. And while also dealing with their retaliations. "There was a lot of that. They started chop blocking! Like [Chicago's head coach] Mike Ditka, that's what he was known for, chop blocking. He'd teach his boys to chop block all the time. [As did former San Francisco 49ers head coach] Bill Walsh," said Manley. "It was legal, but at the same time it was unethical that they'd want to chop block a defensive lineman. And some of the offensive linemen wouldn't do it because they knew it could be career-ending.

"But I think more importantly, the players got frustrated and I think the coaches as well, because I was a motor-mouth. I would talk a lot. And I think it frustrated a lot of people because of the fact that I said what I was going to do and I did it!"

What is perhaps Manley's most famous sack occurred during the 1982 NFC Championship Game against Dallas on January 22, 1983, when, late in the first half, he sacked Danny White, which forced the Cowboys quarterback out of the game because of a concussion.

And then while pressuring White's replacement, Gary Hogeboom, in the fourth quarter, Manley tipped a pass into the hands of Darryl Grant. The defensive tackle returned the interception 10 yards for a touchdown, helping Washington win, 31–17, and move on to Super Bowl XVII.

A Pass-Rushing Mentor

The Redskins, in essence, made a two-for-one deal when they traded a late-round future draft choice to the New England Patriots for Tony McGee just 10 days before the 1982 season opener. Not only were they getting a veteran defensive end, they were also acquiring a mentor for another defensive end who was about to enter into his second season.

"When I heard about the trade, and me being in my 12th year, I didn't know if this was a setup to get me out of the league or if [the Redskins] really needed me," said McGee. "Then [general manager] Bobby Beathard called and said that he had watched me for a long time and that I could really help the team. So I started to feel pretty positive about it. And then I got here, and as a matter of fact, I remember it was the last preseason game and we were playing Cincinnati. That night, I wore No. 60 and didn't even have a name on my back.

"They had lost all the preseason games, and I was kind of looking around at the team and I didn't know what I was looking at. I hadn't heard of a lot of the people. Naturally, I had heard of Joe Theismann. John Riggins and I were in an all-star camp together, so I knew of him. Perry Brooks and I, I was in New England when they drafted him. So they were the three people I knew on the team.

"They told me I'd be a pass-rusher. But I remember later during the year, we were playing the New York Giants, and an assistant coach called me over because he and I had been in New England together. He said, 'You know why they brought you here? They want you to pass rush, but they want you to also help Dexter Manley with his maturity.' And that was Bill Parcells. Dexter was a young and up-and-coming defensive end, and they wanted me to help with him."

They would both help Washington that year. Winning eight of nine games during the strike-shortened season, the Redskins made the play-offs for the first time since 1976. Coincidently, not participating in the postseason was something that McGee was familiar with. During his previous 11 seasons, eight with the Patriots and three with the Chicago Bears, his teams played in just two playoff games—both with New England and both losses.

"It was tremendous because I did not know if I was going to have that opportunity," McGee said. "Before you know it, seven, eight, nine years are gone, and you haven't been in the playoffs. And when I got [to Washington], you'd have to look at it. You walk in, and the team was 0–4 in the preseason, and you know they were 8–8 the year prior to that. You don't know what to expect! I did notice that everybody worked together, everybody worked hard, and everybody worked towards the same goal. People stepped up, and I had no idea they were that talented. It just took off."

And then some. McGee and his teammates notched four victories during the playoffs, capping the season with the Super Bowl XVII championship.

The Redskins Got Their Mann

Drafting Charles Mann in the third round of the 1983 draft out of the casino-laden neighborhood of the University of Nevada–Reno was not really too much of a gamble for the Redskins. He was, after all, the Big Sky Conference's Most Valuable Defensive Lineman in 1981 and 1982.

But even with those trophies adorning his mantle, the defensive end was just hoping for an opportunity to prove himself at the NFL level and explained his reaction to being given that chance by Washington. "Excitement. Elation. Joy. It's something I think that every young man that has aspirations of going and playing professionally [dreams of]. And I accomplished it," said Mann. "I was not a Redskins fan. I grew up in California and was a [Los Angeles] Rams fan, but I didn't care what team I got on. I just wanted to be on a team. So [the fact that the Redskins had captured the Super Bowl XVII title three months earlier] wasn't really the issue. The issue was I made it."

Once in training camp, Mann made it with the help of his new teammates. "The game was totally different than now," he said. "There were always veterans showing young guys the ropes. That's how it was. You didn't move forward without a veteran kind of showing you the way. It was just understood."

In 1985, his second full season as a starter, Mann recorded what would be a career-high 14.5 sacks, the second-highest on the team to Dexter Manley's 15, and the fourth-highest total in the NFC. He added 21 quarterback pressures and 85 tackles. "When you come into the league, you don't know what you don't know. And all of a sudden after a couple of seasons, you begin to understand," Mann said. "And then it doesn't take as much energy to accomplish the same thing."

Following the regular season, three Redskins—offensive linemen Russ Grimm and Joe Jacoby, and receiver Art Monk—were chosen to play in the Pro Bowl. Not Mann. Not any defensive players. Was he surprised? Disappointed? "No, I was excited about what I did," said Mann. "Whether somebody acknowledged it by selecting me to the Pro Bowl is not the issue. The issue is my peers are taking notice."

His peers indeed took notice and sent him to the Pro Bowl three consecutive seasons (1987–1989) and added a fourth trip for good measure in 1991.

Mann played for 11 seasons in Washington and left to conclude his NFL career in 1994 with the San Francisco 49ers with a pair of Super Bowl rings, the four Pro Bowl nods, and 83 sacks. What does he attribute his success wearing the burgundy and gold to?

"Fear of losing a job. [Head coach] Joe Gibbs was really good at instilling that in us," said Mann, who was named by the team as one of the 70 Greatest Redskins in 2002. "These guys nowadays, they don't have that fear because you already get the prize when you arrive and land that huge contract, that prize. So it was dangled in front of us. Most of us never received it, but it was always dangled in front of us, something to motivate us."

"Here for a Reason"

Unable to see eye-to-eye on why his contract should be renegotiated after starting at defensive end the previous two seasons, the Pittsburgh Steelers sent their 1987 sixth-round draft choice Tim Johnson to the Redskins in 1990.

And even though once he arrived in Washington and was given a new position, defensive tackle, and a new role, backup to Darryl Grant and Markus Koch, Johnson had an optimistic attitude. "Really, all I wanted was a chance. I figured if I could get myself in shape and learn the system well enough, I'd become fair game for anybody," said Johnson. "I didn't come with great hopes of taking the starting job and all that. I wanted to just get in the door and get a chance and work hard. One thing I learned in Pittsburgh is how to work hard. Not too many teams work as hard as those guys, but when I got to the Redskins, there was no slack in that. Coach Gibbs definitely knows how to work, as well.

"I knew how to work, so that part of my confidence was, hey, I know what to do. I'm going to come in here and just lay it all on the line. And if it works out, I know the Lord had me here for a reason. And if it doesn't, I have no regrets."

Based on that season's NFC wild-card game victory over Philadelphia, evidently, there was a reason. Johnson made his first start at left tackle for the Redskins and sacked Eagles quarterback Randall Cunningham two times for 16 yards in losses, pressured him into another sack, had five tackles, and forced a fumble. Those individual efforts were recognized when he was named as the NFC Defensive Player of the Week.

"Sometimes you hit a groove as an athlete and you also, for one reason or another, are able to attack against certain offenses more than others," Johnson said. "I think because I wasn't a name player, no one really expected a lot when No. 78 came into the game. I was able to go in almost stealth, under the radar. All of the things that I'd been working on began to bear fruit. You can work on all the techniques and just work hard and then all of a sudden, you hit a groove where you're comfortable. You can just go all out without thinking about it. I think I hit a stride in that game where I was very comfortable. Going to the playoffs, there's another level of intensity. I experienced that."

Sack King

Washington's 2003 season, particularly the second half, was highlight-free. Well, almost highlight-free.

The Redskins, at 4–8, went to a bitterly cold Giants Stadium on December 7, looking to win only their second game since late September and securely place New York, also 4–8, in the basement of the NFC East. Nineteen-year veteran Bruce Smith, meanwhile, hoped for a victory over the Giants as well as a sack.

In his fourth year as a Redskin, after spending 15 seasons with the Buffalo Bills, Smith began the afternoon tied with former Eagles and Packers star Reggie White for the NFL's career sacks record with 198. He came close to claiming the mark in the third quarter when he hit quarterback Kerry Collins during a play in which the Giants were penalized for delay of game.

After being bent backward by the defensive end, Collins was forced to leave the game with a high ankle sprain. "It wasn't my intention to hurt Kerry," said Smith. "It was my intention to knock the heck out of him."

Smith took sole possession of the league's all-time record with his 199th career sack with 8:33 remaining in the fourth quarter. Lined up across from second-year veteran Ian Allen, Smith faked outside and then slipped inside the left tackle and pulled down backup quarterback Jesse Palmer by his left ankle for a seven-yard loss.

"I know I'm not in second place any longer," Smith said following the 20–7 victory. "When they print up the football cards, they won't say, 'Second place.' I was rushing outside pretty much all day. [Allen] overstepped. That's a cardinal sin because I have a very good inside move. The quarterback was sitting right there, and I tried to lunge at him. Good things happen to individuals when teams win.

"I don't know what to feel like. I have been playing this game a long time. I've had a lot of surgeries. A lot of very important people were instrumental in prolonging my career."

Smith recorded his 200th [29 as a Redskin and 171 while he played for the Bills] and final sack two games later, on December 21 in Chicago, when he brought down Bears quarterback Rex Grossman during a 27–24 loss.

Retiring at the end of the 2003 season, Smith was inducted in his first year of eligibility into the Pro Football Hall of Fame in 2009.

The $100 Million Man

Two-time All-Pro defensive tackle Albert Haynesworth does not have to be convinced that timing is everything. Just two months after recording a career-high 8.5 sacks, to go along with 51 tackles, 22 quarterback pressures, and four forced fumbles for the Tennessee Titans in 2008, he became a free agent, a member of the Redskins, and incredibly wealthy all in the same day.

When free agency opened on February 27, 2009, Haynesworth became the NFL's highest-paid defensive player by signing a record seven-year, $100 million contract with Washington. The deal includes $41 million in guarantees, the highest total in league history.

"With the contract, it's going to be all on me," said the 6'6", 320-pound Haynesworth. "What they want me to come here and do is play football and be disruptive, do what I do, so that's what I've come here to do. When you get on the field, you're not thinking about dollar signs or anything like that, you're just going out there to play. It's a lot of money, but honestly, I put more pressure on myself than what the contract will do.

"I have such high standards for myself that, you know, [the Redskins] can pay me half a billion dollars, and it still would have been

The Redskins signed free agent and All-Pro defensive tackle Albert Haynesworth to a seven-year contract in 2009 that included $41 million in guarantees.

the pressure I put on myself. I expect myself to play at a high level and to dominate. And if I'm not making plays, then people around me are making plays. As far as the number, I mean, yeah, it's great, it's awesome, don't get me wrong. But as far as the pressure, no."

With seven years of pro experience, all with the Titans, Haynesworth vowed that he would not go down in Redskins lore as a "bust" but instead make opposing offensive linemen's lives miserable on game days. "When I line up in front of somebody, put that helmet on, it's to kick butt," Haynesworth said. "It's to make sure that guy knows that I'm the best player he played against. After the game, you can think about the money. But during that game, I'm going to make sure he knows that I'm the best player. Any team that faces me, they're going to have to worry about me.

"If you look at my game, I'm a player who goes straight forward. I'm a disruptive player and I can take on the double team to free up other [teammates]. I want to be able to attack my guy, make plays, and allow everyone else to make plays off me."

chapter 11

Tackles, Hits, and Blitzes

If You Can't Beat Him, Trade for Him

Drafted by the New York Giants in 1956, Sam Huff was a key reason why over the next eight seasons, they made it to six NFL Championship Games, winning the title in 1956. A four-time Pro Bowl linebacker, he was also a major reason why the Giants held a 13–2–1 record against their division rival Redskins during that same period.

Thus you can imagine his, well, let's just say disappointment upon learning that he had been traded to Washington in 1964 for running back Dick James and defensive tackle Andy Stynchula. "I was ticked off! I had my family in New York, we were settled, I owned a house, and I had a job in the off-season. I had everything set for the future. It was all there," said Huff. "I was happy being a Giant. We had, I believe, the best defense ever put together in the NFL. Or one of them, anyway.

"[Giants head coach] Allie Sherman called my wife, I was in Cleveland on a business trip. Mary called and said that she just received a call and that I was traded to the Washington Redskins and that I should be real happy because he got two players for me."

Sherman's counterpart with the Redskins, Bill McPeak, who was more than likely much happier, chose to leave his telephone on its hook to discuss the deal with Huff face-to-face. "He came to New York to sign me and talk with me and tell me I could have my shirt, No. 70, with the Redskins," Huff said. "And that he needed me to be the leader of the defense and that we're going to have two key players, me and [quarterback] Sonny [Jurgensen, whom Washington had acquired in a trade with Philadelphia that year]. Sonny would run the offense, and I'd run the defense. [McPeak] really needed the leadership, and being the Pro Bowl player that I was, and the quarterback that Sonny was, he felt that we could make a difference."

The coach was right. Huff and Jurgensen did make a difference. In that first season, they helped the Redskins improve to a 6–8 record, twice as many victories as the previous season.

"Well, we had a pretty good defensive record. Sonny did not have the talent [on offense] that we had," said Huff, who was chosen to play in his fifth Pro Bowl. "We had a Pro Bowl player in John Paluck, who was a great defensive end. We had two great tackles to work with: Joe Rutgens and Bob Toneff. They transferred Carl Kammerer, who was a linebacker, to defensive end. And we had Paul Krause, who was a great rookie, who played safety. He had [a league-leading] 12 interceptions. We had Lonnie Sanders as a corner and Johnny Sample as the other corner. And we had Jim Steffen, who was a great tackler, as a strong-side safety. He was almost like a linebacker. So we put together a pretty good defensive unit. We ranked in the top five in the NFL.

"The worst part about when I came to the Redskins, to be honest with you, they had no front office. They had four people in the front office. That's it. And they had no receivers coach. Bill McPeak was a great guy, but he had all his friends as assistant coaches and different things."

A Steal That Turned Into a Star

As the head coach, Bill McPeak guided the Redskins to only 15 victories out of 56 games prior to when the NFL held its 1965 draft. He'd make up for it that day by selecting North Carolina's Chris Hanburger in the 18th round, 245th overall.

It wasn't a steal. It was larceny. Grand larceny.

"I was surprised I even got drafted," said Hanburger. "I had no intentions of playing professional football. I didn't know anything about it. I did it in college only because it was a means to an end in the sense that it was a scholarship. By playing, I could get an education. I didn't even know very much at all about professional football."

After reporting to Washington's training camp, Hanburger received a crash course on how to play the game from 10-year veteran Sam Huff. He was a fast learner even if he didn't always agree with the standout linebacker and moved into the starting lineup 10 games into the season. "He used to be critical of me tackling high, and I told him the reason I did that was so I wouldn't get hurt," Hanburger said. "And I'll never forget, in fact, I think he has a picture in his house of me bending over him after he stuck his head into a big fullback up in Pittsburgh and got put into la-la land. I looked down at him and told him, 'That's why you don't stick your head into someone, Sam. You tackle high!'"

Hanburger tackled high and often, and the following year was selected to play in the Pro Bowl for first of nine times. "Anytime you get recognized for anything, it's awfully nice," said Hanburger, who was named All-NFL three times and was the 1972 NFC Defensive Player of the Year. "I don't know why [I was chosen to play in the Pro Bowl so often] because there certainly were a lot of real good linebackers when I played. But I always had a lot of respect for the fact the other players on other teams thought enough about the way I played to vote me into that game."

Nine trips to the Pro Bowl out of 14 seasons with the Redskins, Hanburger played in 187 games and finished his career with 19 interceptions and 17 fumble recoveries, three of which he returned for touchdowns. A strong case could be made that he's worthy of Hall of Fame consideration.

"It's no big deal for me. I guess I'm probably a little different than a lot of people," Hanburger said. "I'm certainly not going to lose any sleep over it because I guess I don't understand the process. Even if I did, it wouldn't change my opinion of the way I feel about it. I just think there are an awful lot of people that aren't in it that certainly deserve to be in it. And I'm not saying that I deserve to be in there by any means. I just look at it as something that if it happens, it happens. If it doesn't, who cares?

"For someone that plays—I think you have to be retired five years before you can go in—now for somebody like that, I think it's fantastic because that guy can certainly enjoy it. I mean, he's only been away five years; he's probably still involved with thought and everything else. It's just a wonderful thing. But in my case, heck, I've never even thought about it, worried about it, or anything else. And never will.

"I can respect people saying, 'Well, the people that followed you when you played, they'd really love to see something like that happen for you.' It's just my opinion, but I think the older you get, to me anyway, the less significance it has. I think when I retired, I put it behind me."

Huff's Encore

As reliable as duct tape and as sturdy as a telephone pole, five-time Pro Bowl linebacker Sam Huff was in the NFL for 11-plus seasons, 154 games, before he was sent to Washington's sideline in 1967. "That was the only four games I ever missed in my entire 13-year career. What happened was, they drafted a big ol' tackle by the name of Spain Musgrove, who did not really want to be a football player. He wanted to be a clothes designer," said Huff. "We were playing in Los Angeles and [Rams quarterback] Roman Gabriel—the hardest guy for me to ever tackle because he never knew where he was running and I didn't know where he was running—and so I tackled him and my foot is sticking out. Spain Musgrove, trying to get in on the tackle, fell on my foot. He weighed about 270 pounds and just tore all the ligaments and tendons in my ankle. It would have been better off if it would have broken."

Huff decided to retire prior to the 1968 campaign, not because of the ankle injury, but because he wasn't too happy with the Redskins' coaching staff.

"They fired Bill McPeak [before the 1966 season] and brought in Otto Graham," Huff said. "Otto Graham, I hate to say it, he basically didn't have control. I don't know. It just wasn't working, and so I thought it was time for me to retire."

His retirement plans were interrupted because of a fateful plane trip when he sat near a legendary coach named Vince Lombardi, who was about to fill out a change-of-address form. "We were going to the Super Bowl, and I was heading up a group down in New Orleans," said Huff. "He was a coach with the New York Giants when I was there, and so we were good friends. He and his wife were on the airplane, and we started talking, and I said, 'I read in the paper where you'll probably coach the Redskins.' And he said, 'Well, you know, that rumor is probably true.' I said, 'If you do, I want to come and be involved with your defense.'

"So when he signed a deal [with Washington on February 7, 1969], he hired Harland Svare, who was a teammate of mine [with the Giants] who was coaching defense then. He was let go by the Giants, and Lombardi hired him [as] defensive coordinator. And so I became the linebackers coach and a player, a player/coach. I worked with the linebackers and I enjoyed that. I enjoyed the time on the field, particularly working with Chris Hanburger. It was a great experience for me, but it was a lot of hard work doing everything the coaches did and then everything the players did, too."

That was Huff's final year of a spectacular career, and he was inducted into the Pro Football Hall of Fame in 1982.

Following the Leader

Jack Pardee was raised in Texas and played for 13 seasons in the NFL with the Los Angeles Rams. But when his head coach of five years, George Allen, headed to Washington in 1971, even though he had no familiarity with the East Coast, the linebacker aspired to join him. Allen had similar feelings and traded for the veteran.

"I was a player/coach back then, a deal I'd worked out with George," said Pardee. "And with him leaving, I wanted to go with him as a coach, or as a player, or whatever. I was going to be leaving the Rams. If they hadn't worked out a trade, I was going to retire. I didn't want to be playing for someone else. He meant everything to me."

With the talk of retiring put on hold, Pardee was joined in Washington by, among others, former Rams Diron Talbert, Richie Petitbon, and Myron Pottios. He continued his coach-on-the-field persona and helped the Redskins open the season with five straight wins and compile a 9–4–1 record, the team's highest number of victories since they won 10 games in 1942.

"It was a real fun experience. And the fans in Washington, after being in Los Angeles with the blasé fans, as many of them rooted for the opposing team as the home team, were really a breath of fresh air. And to have the immediate success was a great experience," said Pardee.

"The fun that we were having with the group that George had put together, getting Diron Talbert, Ron McDole, Verlon Biggs, defensively; they had done a big rebuilding job. Of course, there was a good group left over, too, in Pat Fischer, Mike Bass, and Chris Hanburger. There was about half left over and half a new group that blended together beautifully. We had fun working out, we had fun on the practice field, and we had fun playing."

If the 1971 campaign was fun, the following season with an 11–3 record and the NFC championship title could have been considered a riot. Well, that was up until Super Bowl VII when the Redskins fell to the destiny-bound, undefeated Miami Dolphins.

"We were the last team to beat them, in a preseason game [27–24 on August 31] at RFK Stadium," Pardee said. "By doing that, we really felt good going in that we could handle them. Unfortunately, the worst game we played that year was in the Super Bowl."

A Linebacker's Back and In Charge

With 15 years of experience (two in Washington) as a player and player/coach, and one season as an assistant coach, also with the Redskins, Jack Pardee followed his mentor George Allen's footsteps in 1975 and became a head coach himself when he accepted the top job with the Chicago Bears. "I'd end up changing some terminology, and we didn't necessarily use the same offensive or defensive plays, but the way you go about preparing, I tried to do primarily the same thing he did," said Pardee.

When Allen left Washington three years later and its head coaching job became available, Pardee could not blow out of the Windy City fast enough. He became the 16th head coach in Redskins history on January 24, 1978. "In Chicago at that time, we were playing at Soldier Field, and they were getting ready to condemn it because of infrastructure and everything else," said Pardee, who was 20–22 with the Bears. "We didn't have a workout facility after Thanksgiving [because of the weather]. We managed to make the playoffs [in 1977], but I saw us having a hard time trying to get any further with the situation there.

"In Washington with Edward Bennett Williams [as the owner], whatever you needed to win, the team was able to get. And even though we didn't have many draft choices, I thought we could get by until we get in the draft again. With the conditions and situations, I thought we'd have a better chance to succeed than in Chicago."

Not having many draft choices was not an exaggeration. Allen had dealt numerous picks away in previous trades. Washington's first selection in the 1978 draft didn't occur until the sixth round.

Nevertheless, under Pardee, the Redskins opened the 1978 season with six consecutive victories, their best start in 35 years. They, however, only managed to win two more games over the course of the remaining schedule and finished at 8–8.

"It was a little bit scheduling, and we were winning close games," Pardee said. "Mike Thomas was having a real good season [before he was injured] in the fifth or sixth game, so we lost a running back and all of a sudden, we started losing those one-point games. We had a running back that was having an All-Pro-type year at the time, and we just didn't get him replaced."

In 1979 Pardee led Washington to a 10–6 record and was named as the NFL Coach of the Year by the Associated Press. But there was no chance of winning the award back-to-back after the team went 6–10 in 1980. Needless to say, he and then-owner Jack Kent Cooke were disappointed. And something that may have made Pardee's job even more difficult was a strained relationship with general manager Bobby Beathard.

"I hired him. And then I guess he made a hit with the owner and things changed," said Pardee. "Yeah, it disappointed me, but that's life. It was just like any coach and whoever makes personnel decisions. My third year there, Beathard wouldn't re-sign [tight end] Jean Fugett or [receiver] Danny Buggs, and [running back John] Riggins wasn't there [because of a contract dispute]. I mean, gol' darn, who are we going to have on offense? All our production from the year before, it wasn't there."

Cooke relieved Pardee of his duties on January 5, 1981, and replaced him with Joe Gibbs.

No Time to Think Twice

Six of Washington's first eight picks in the 1979 draft were dealt away even before representatives from the NFL teams gathered in New York to make selections. The Redskins, nevertheless, scored with the two choices they still had left by taking tight end Don Warren in the fourth round and Penn State linebacker Rich Milot in the seventh.

The former Nittany Lion impressed head coach Jack Pardee, a former linebacker himself, enough during training camp to be put in the starting lineup for the season opener against Houston. "He seemed to have a fair amount of confidence [in me]," said Milot. "It was just preparing like any other game. It was more your teammates that were riding you a little bit."

Milot, meanwhile, was more concerned about being run over when the team took the field at RFK Stadium. "The first game I started was against [5'11", 232-pound running back/fullback/human tank] Earl Campbell, and I was scared to death! You watch the films, and he was running over everybody. You don't get scared to death, but I don't think you want him to embarrass you, run you over, and do one of those things."

Surviving Campbell, Milot remained in Washington's lineup and would make six more starts in what turned out to be a crash-course-like rookie campaign. "Actually, I had a good preseason, so I wasn't surprised [to be starting] initially. But looking back, it may have been one of the worst things to happen to me, to be honest with you. Being that, I don't think I was ready for it," Milot said. "Really, my only experience as a defensive player was at Penn State. I think I had maybe five, six, seven games under my belt. And the preseason's a lot different. It's very simple. When you get into the [regular-season] games, plans are a little bit more complicated. I don't know if I was ready to start yet. At some point it'd be easier I think or a little bit better if you could just be worked in."

The 12ᵗʰ Starter

By playing in 216 games for the Redskins, Monte Coleman proved that a player doesn't have to be an early-round draft choice to be a team leader. And that one doesn't have to be a Pro Bowler to be a star in the National Football League.

Being selected in the 11th round of the 1979 college draft, 289th overall, did not weaken the linebacker's aspiration to make the roster. "I wasn't really concerned about what round [I was chosen in the draft], I more or less just wanted an opportunity," said Coleman. "That was my main concern, just to have an opportunity. I was going to make the most of it."

That, he did. Wearing Washington's burgundy and gold for 16 seasons, Coleman credits his belief and his work ethic as the key reasons for his longevity in the league. "I was extremely blessed, and I mean that sincerely. God really had a plan for me. And my workout ethics off the field really had a lot to do with it. Normally, we would have to report to start training around the 15th of March. My due date was always the 1st of February. I always got a little ahead of everybody as far as conditioning. My philosophy was: if I don't get out of shape, I won't need to get into shape. It's hard to get in shape, but it's easy to maintain.

"What I did was maintain. I was a team player. If there was something to be done on the field, the coaches knew they could count on me. I went out and tried to do it."

That was Coleman's way of thinking, regardless if he was starting or not. "It was no different. I considered myself a starter," he said. "Coaches came up to me several times and said, 'The reason that you're not starting is because you're too valuable to the team in other areas.' So I took that as a compliment. The only down that I really missed pretty much through my whole career was first down. Neal Olkewicz played first down and other people [did so] after he left. But normally, I was there for second and third downs, which were passing situations. So I was kind of the 12th man in a sense on a 12-man starting defense."

Suiting up for the Redskins from 1979 through 1994, Coleman, along with Donnie Warren and Sammy Baugh, were the only three players to play in three decades for Washington. (Twenty-year veteran Darrell Green joined the list after he retired following the 2002 season.) Coleman played under four different head coaches—Jack Pardee, Joe Gibbs, Richie Petitbon, and Norv Turner—and saw the NFL grow... literally.

"Guys started getting bigger, getting faster," said Coleman. "And the competition around the league, they asked for parity, and sure enough at the end of my career, parity was definitely there. You really only had a couple of dominant teams, but they were being phased out, pretty much.

"In the league itself, I don't think the loyalty to players was there. You won't see another Darrell Green around the league, where he comes to one team and plays there his entire career. So the loyalty of players and owners went away. It was almost like it changed from being a sport to a business."

Go Ahead and Just Try to Get Him off the Field

Because he didn't have the prototypical size for a middle linebacker on paper, there may have been some hesitancy about whether the 6', 230-pound Neal Olkewicz could play in the NFL. But once he stepped on the field as a rookie free agent at Washington's 1979 training camp, any uncertainty disappeared faster than $10 laying on a sidewalk in Times Square.

Having been raised outside of Philadelphia and having gone to the University of Maryland, Olkewicz was keenly aware of the Redskins' tradition and admits that he was somewhat intimidated to share the huddle with veterans such as Diron Talbert and Ken Houston.

"I think everybody's a little bit in awe to be with the pros, people that you've watched on TV and heard about," said Olkewicz. "[I was fortunate that] a lot of guys kind of took me under their wing. They seemed to like the way I played and kind of took me in."

After Olkewicz made the roster and contributed mostly on special teams, Washington's coach Jack Pardee put him in at linebacker during the season's seventh game on October 14, which was against the Browns in Cleveland. "They just basically decided that the last couple of games, the defense in general against the run hadn't done real well. So I think they kind of made up their minds that if it didn't get turned around, they were going to try something.

"About after a quarter, they replaced Don Hover, who was the starting linebacker, with me. [The coaches] just told me to go in, and I played the rest of the game. I just remember being excited. I made a lot of tackles and we won the game [13–9], and I started from then on."

That game in Cleveland was basically the beginning. Olkewicz would be in the starting lineup for 137 regular-season and three Super Bowl games during his 11 years with Washington. Defensive tackle Dave Butz, his teammate for 10 of those seasons, feels that even though Olkewicz didn't get acknowledged by making a Pro Bowl, he was a key reason why the Redskins were so successful.

"Neal was phenomenal," said Butz. "Neal was a fantastic player, had a great heart, wanted to play football, and didn't want to come off the field. I can remember a couple of times in the huddle when we used to trade guys in and out [as specialty substitutions], and he'd say, 'Damn it! Get me some guys that can play all downs!'"

"That's true! Sometimes I would cuss at them when I was leaving, too," laughed Olkewicz. "Like most guys, I would love to play every down. But in reality, it probably helped me play longer. That's the way the game had evolved. It became much more of a chess match.

"I just had a love for the game. I enjoyed what I did and I enjoyed showing people that they were wrong, that I could make it. With my size and speed, I wasn't really expected by anybody to be more than a special-teams player if I made it at all. So it was kind of nice to show everybody."

Heading to a Home He'd Never Seen

Few would have blamed Joe Gibbs or any of Washington's college scouts after the first day of the 1990 NFL Draft if they had made a quick stop on the way home to buy a scratch-off lottery ticket. Owning only one pick out of the first 75, the Redskins were on a lucky roll after they chose Penn State's All-America linebacker Andre Collins in the second round, 46th overall.

Even though he was raised in Cinnaminson, New Jersey, with his 18 brothers and sisters, Collins felt in a way that he was heading home. "I remember being relieved that I was going to a winning franchise, a franchise that had had a great history," said Collins, who recorded a career-high 130 tackles as a senior with the Nittany Lions, the third highest total in the school's history. "I was thrilled because, growing up in New Jersey, outside Philadelphia, the Eagles were always blacked out because they never sold out the stadium. So we always had the Redskins games [on television], and I'll tell you, 85 percent of my family were diehard Redskins fans before I'd even put on a Redskins uniform, including myself."

Considering that only one player, Darrell Green, had started every game as a rookie during the Gibbs era, the odds were greater than 85 percent that Collins wouldn't be the second. But hold the dice. Fourth-year veteran Ravin Caldwell held out of training camp in a contract dispute, which opened the door for Collins. He barged through it and was in the starting lineup on the first day of the preseason.

"I got drafted high so I felt like they were going to give me every opportunity to make the team," Collins said. "But to come into a team like the Redskins, with so much talent...at the time you're talking about Wilber Marshall, Ravin Caldwell, Monte Coleman, and Kurt Gouveia. I didn't really expect to play right away. But one thing people don't under-stand about the NFL is that playing time is situational.

"My abilities just matched up with what the Redskins were trying to do at that particular time. And because it was situational, I had an opportunity to play and start. I was grateful for that. I don't think that I was any better than anyone that we had there, just something that I did allowed them to put me on the field. The timing was just right."

Appreciating and Making History

Beginning in 1988, his first year with the then-Phoenix Cardinals, and through the next four seasons, eight of the 10 times that outside line-backer Ken Harvey played against the Redskins, he left the field in not exactly a celebratory mood.

But in 1993 Washington was swept in the two games against its division rivals, and, well, Harvey was the one holding a broom.

In the first meeting between the teams on September 12 at RFK Stadium, he recorded three sacks and forced a fumble in the 17–10 victory. A little over a month later on October 17 in Arizona, Harvey contributed to the 36–6 win with another sack and forced fumble. As it would turn out, nearly half of his season's 9.5 sacks came against the bur-gundy and gold.

And so when Harvey became a free agent in 1994, those two colors added with green, as in money—a reported $11 million over four years—and the team's history, made the Redskins look very attractive in his eyes. "Originally, I had tried to go back to the Cardinals, but it was contract time, and you start looking around at the different teams," said Harvey. "I knew of the tradition of the Redskins. They kind of kicked our butts [nearly] every time we played against them, so I was like, this could be a good team even though they were on the downswing. I thought they had potential to come back around. History and, honestly, they offered a nice salary. It was a good location. It just seemed like the right move."

Indeed it was, for Harvey and the Redskins. During his first season in Washington, Harvey came through with nine sacks in the final 10 games and, along with Minnesota's John Randle, co-led the NFC with a career-high 13.5 sacks. In addition, Harvey led the team with 20 quarterback hurries and four forced fumbles.

"For me, it was always, you've been given that opportunity and now you have to go in there and show them why they took a gamble on you and how it's going to pay off. That was kind of my attitude. I wanted to prove that they made the right move."

Harvey feels that he owes part of his success to his surroundings, more specifically, to his teammates. "[Veteran linebacker] Monte Coleman would always give me pointers and tips. And [defensive end] Tim Johnson, after I'd make a play, I would come off to the sideline and he would tell me to try this or what I was doing wrong. So that was kind of big," Harvey said. "And then in practice, I had [offensive tackle] Jim Lachey, and he would give me techniques. He would beat me half the time, but then he would explain why he beat me. And so it was the combination of all that that just really elevated my game."

Besides breaking Coleman's team record for sacks by a linebacker, Harvey also became only the fourth one in NFC history to lead the conference in the category and earned what would be his first of four consecutive trips to the Pro Bowl.

"I was excited because all my years in Phoenix, I think I played well. Well enough to get to the Pro Bowl and never got there. I was so excited I bought the whole defensive team watches," laughed Harvey. "Before

Washington, you'd read in some of the magazines, and they said, 'One of the most underrated players,' and stuff like that. But that doesn't do you a whole lot of good when you read you're underrated. It's because nobody's watching you. But I came to Washington, and the games are on [national] TV, and we had this huge fan base. The fans loved you, and so it was a great feeling."

chapter 12

Secondary to None

A Quarterback's Nightmare

During his high school days in Michigan, Paul Krause earned all-state accolades in football, baseball, basketball, and track. And as a two-sport standout at the University of Iowa, he played defensive back and receiver in football and was a center fielder on the Hawkeyes' baseball team. He, however, chose to forgo the possibility of a career on the diamond and was excited when the Redskins chose him in the second round of the 1964 NFL Draft.

"My initial reaction was, 'Great!' The Washington Redskins were one of the original NFL teams, and the D.C. area was an attractive area for me to go to," Krause said. "I was [also] drafted by the [AFL's] Denver Broncos, and at that point, I was an All-America baseball player. Denver said that they would have let me play baseball, too. But at that point, I think that I was more interested in seeing if I could make it in the NFL."

Newsflash: he could. In his first game for the Redskins on September 13 against Cleveland, he swiped two of seventh-year veteran quarterback Frank Ryan's passes. The free safety gathered 10 more interceptions during the course of the season, including a pick in a record-setting seven consecutive games. The rookie's 12 interceptions led the league and secured him a unanimous spot on the All-NFL team.

"I always felt that I was good enough to make some contributions. It probably surprised me that I became an All-Pro my rookie year. And I have to put this in context, [veteran linebacker] Sam Huff always said that he made me my rookie year," laughed Krause. "Sam took the credit, and I do have to give him some of the credit. [Setting the record for interceptions in seven straight games is] where Sam thinks he took the credit. He put me in the right spot at the right time. And I can remember some instances that he probably did. But as far as me catching the ball and everything, I thought I had the ability to do that. Seven interceptions in seven straight games was pretty good. Twelve in a season was pretty good."

Few would argue that. And Krause feels that, regardless of Washington's 6–8 record in each of his first two seasons, a look around the locker room confirmed that he was in "pretty good" company, as well.

"I was a rookie that didn't really understand what was going on the first couple years. I'm just out there trying to play as well as I can play and make the team and help the team," said Krause, who collected six more interceptions during his second season. "As I look back on it now, we had some great football players there. Bobby Mitchell's in the Hall of Fame. Sonny Jurgensen's in the Hall of Fame. Sam Huff's in the Hall of Fame. Charley Taylor's in the Hall of Fame. And I'm in the Hall of Fame. Why we didn't play better as a football team? I have no idea."

Notch One More Loss for the Cowboys

Fortunately for Brig Owens and the Redskins, Dallas Cowboys head coach Tom Landry did not consider any rivalry or potential rivalry when he dealt the young safety to Washington in 1966. "They traded me here [for veteran safety Jim Steffen and a draft choice] which was the best thing that ever happened to me," said Owens. "I said, 'Thank you very much.' Because at that time in Dallas, there were a lot of places that the black ballplayers couldn't eat and places we couldn't stay. So it was very frustrating for me. I was glad when they said they were going to trade me. Landry told me [later] it was one of the biggest mistakes he ever made."

What turned out to not be a mistake was when Landry decided that Owens, a quarterback at the University of Cincinnati, would flourish better at a different position. "He said, 'You're a great athlete, we've got to find a place for you to play,'" Owens said. "He tried me out at wide receiver, a little bit at running back, and then he put me at defensive back. I said, 'I've never played defense. I've never even tackled anyone before.'

"On my first tackle, I ended up having 11 or 12 stitches over my eyebrow. It was in a nutcracker drill. And Amos Marsh was one of the great, big fullbacks. Marsh was about 235, 240, and he had thighs as big as my body. All I knew was I had to hit him in the numbers, pick him up, and take him down. I went through and hit him, picked him up, and took him down. And when I got up, I saw stars and at the same time what I thought was sweat was [actually] blood. I said, 'This is not for me.'"

Well, Owens was wrong. He would learn how to tackle and he would definitely learn how to come up with interceptions. He actually proved to be a lightning quick study in regards to the latter. "I got [to Washington] and the first game I played [the 1966 preseason finale against Philadelphia], I intercepted two balls [off of Eagles quarterback Norm Snead] and ran one back for a touchdown," said Owens. "Pete Retzlaff, who was one of the premier tight ends at the time, I shut him down, and I started [for first-year head coach Otto Graham] from that point on."

Beginning with a team-high seven interceptions as a rookie, Owens would lead the Redskins in picks three of his first five seasons, totaling 23. He'd also total three head coaches during that same timeframe: Graham, Vince Lombardi, and Bill Austin. George Allen became his fourth when he took over the Redskins in 1971. The following year, they compiled an 11–3 record, earned the NFC championship, and made their way to Super Bowl VII.

"It all started out under Lombardi in terms of creating camaraderie," said Owens, who would collect 36 interceptions and return three for touchdowns during his 12 seasons with the Redskins. "George Allen took it to another level in terms of camaraderie and that we were really, truly a family and together. But also, we had a group of players that some teams didn't want or were afraid to have. George sort of said, 'It's us against the league. It's us against the world.' And so everyone bought into that. We spent a lot of time together at Redskin Park and had what they called the 'Friday Afternoon Club.' So we were a very close-knit group.

"Take for instance when George Allen got inducted into the Hall of Fame [in 2002]. We had 34 or 35 guys show up [in Canton, Ohio] for that. That had never happened before!"

More of a Gift Than a Trade

As a rookie free safety in 1964, Paul Krause set a league record when he gathered an interception in seven consecutive games. He finished the season atop the NFL with 12 picks.

He led the Redskins again the next year with six interceptions and was selected to play in the Pro Bowl for a second straight season. And over the next two campaigns, Krause collected 10 more for a total of 28 interceptions in his first four seasons.

And then unexpectedly in 1968, Washington traded him to Minnesota for linebacker Marlin McKeever and a future draft choice. "I was very surprised about the trade to the Vikings," said Krause. "Although [because of] the relationship I had with the defensive backfield coach, that trade didn't surprise me. Ed Hughes was the coach and he wanted me to be more like a linebacker. And at 6'4", 200 pounds, I was not that type of player. My first year: 12 interceptions. My second year: six interceptions. My goodness, those were numbers that nobody in the league had seen before. And why somebody would want to change that type of football player is beyond me. I think the guy made a very, very foolish judgment on the type of player I was."

The Vikings, on the other hand, could not have made a more astute deal. A fixture in their secondary for the next 12 seasons, Krause added 53 more interceptions to his résumé for a total of 81, and retired following the 1979 campaign as the NFL's all-time interception leader. He was inducted into the Pro Football Hall of Fame in 1998.

"I think I had natural ability because I don't think a guy could do some of those things and set records…the record I have for the 81 interceptions, nobody's really close to that," said Krause, an eight-time Pro Bowler. "You have to have some natural ability, but you have to understand the game of football. You have to understand what your own abilities are and what your opponents' abilities are. I understood what the

with trips to the Pro Bowl. And while he was considered by many NFL followers as the premier strong safety in the game at that time, Houston did not feel that he was a natural. But instead, he felt that he evolved into becoming a star at the position. "In college [at Prairie View A&M], I was an offensive center and a middle linebacker, so I had the ability to hit and I was used to playing inside with the linemen. So I didn't have any fear of having to go up against those guys," said Houston. "But because of my quickness, I adapted well to having to play against a tight end even though it was a position I had to learn the rest of my career because I only started playing the strong safety position in my rookie year of pro ball [1967 with Houston].

"I think [being successful as a strong safety] was a combination of the size that I had and the quickness along with the ability to play inside."

Houston did not have many opportunities to play in the postseason for Washington. With only three playoff appearances—in 1973 against Minnesota, in 1974 against the Los Angeles Rams, and in 1976 versus the Vikings again—each time the Redskins were one and done. Disappointed that he never played in a Super Bowl? "I didn't think about it that much at the time because you always think that you're going to play in one," Houston said. "I would have loved to have gone to a Super Bowl. I think that's probably the one thing in my career that's missing, not having a Super Bowl ring. I'm not jealous, but I see guys with those big rings, and I wish that I had earned one."

What Houston did earn was a spot in the Pro Football Hall of Fame. A 14-year veteran, he finished his career with 49 interceptions, 24 collected as a Redskin, and was enshrined in 1986. "It was a very fast weekend. You have to go back the next year to enjoy what happened. I think the thing about the Hall of Fame is the older you get, the more you realize how important it is in your life," said Houston.

"I made it on the first ballot and I was thinking this is the way it always is. But you see guys that have been out [of the league] for 20 to 25 years and barely getting in. You realize how lucky you are with all of the players who are out there. A lot of guys meet the requirements of being in the Hall of Fame, but they only pick so many. Every year you've got a new crop coming out, so it scares you to death once you look back at it. It's not important in the scheme of life, but in terms of football, it's the most significant award you can get."

Stowing Away a Safety

There's no question that George Allen was a successful coach and renowned for trading draft choices for veteran players. However, evidenced by how he acquired Colgate safety Mark Murphy in 1977, Allen was also a little on the sneaky side. "They've changed the rule since then, but the NFL allowed you to fly people in before the draft or while the draft was going on," said Murphy. "The Redskins called me on the first day of the draft, it was held over two days then, and said, 'Mark, we're going to draft you and we want you here for publicity reasons.' So they flew me down, and I figured they'd take me to the press conference and unveil me as their draft pick.

"Come to find out, what they were doing was hiding me out. There were four or five of us, and they would drive us around town and show us the sights. We had no idea what was going on. Meanwhile, I called my girlfriend, who's my wife now, up at Colgate, and she said, 'Where the heck have you been? I've been calling for hours trying to get through to you!' The hotel phone number that I gave her, they said, 'No, there's no Mark Murphy staying here.' The Redskins had given them instructions to say that.

"They took a gamble that I wouldn't be drafted and they wanted to have me right there. And so as soon as the draft ended, they pulled into Redskins Park and said, 'Here's the deal. You have to sign it.'"

Granted, Washington was deceitful, and as an undrafted rookie, Murphy could have signed a free-agent contract with any other team in the league. But he nevertheless agreed to the deal that the Redskins offered him. "The reason I signed is that I believed they were the only team that wanted me to play safety. Everybody else wanted to try to put some weight on me and move me to linebacker," Murphy said. "I really felt a lot more comfortable playing safety. And the other thing is they were the only team that had sent an actual coach to work me out. It was Ralph Hawkins. I liked Ralph and I really liked the fact that he would be my position coach. I felt like the Redskins had the most interest in me."

The Apprentice

Donald Trump could not have offered a better apprenticeship. After signing with Washington as a rookie free agent in 1977, safety Mark Murphy spent the next two seasons playing behind and learning the nuances of the game from seasoned veterans Ken Houston and Jake Scott.

"You learn a lot about the type of work that's required to be success-ful. Whether it's working out or studying," said Murphy. "You learn a lot of little tricks, especially at a position like safety, that were invaluable to me. And to have the opportunity to play right next to Kenny for two or three years was really great."

The first game that Murphy started alongside Houston was the 1979 season opener against the Houston Oilers and their bruising running back Earl Campbell. "I was very nervous, obviously. Houston was very good then. That was when they had things rolling," Murphy said. "And I remember [one hit on Campbell] vividly. It was late in the game, and they ran a draw play from about the 8-yard line. Unfortunately, or fortunately, I was the only one that read the play, and he had quite a head of steam up and [we met at] about the 1-yard line. As a defensive back, normally when you get somebody like an Earl Campbell, you'd hit them low. But when they're at the 1-yard line, if you hit them low, they'll just go over you and score. So I knew that I had to try to hit him high to knock him backwards. But either gravity or things were not to be on that one.

"He had a relatively short career because he took such a beating, but boy, when he was at his best, he was a load to bring down."

By leading the Redskins in tackles four consecutive seasons (1979–1982), Murphy would bring down a load of loads and was an acknowledged team leader. Washington's NFL Players Association repre-sentative, he was also a team captain during the 1982 and 1983 Super Bowl seasons. "I took it very seriously, especially under coach [Joe] Gibbs," Murphy said. "There was a lot of excitement, and we really felt that we had the opportunity to be successful. I was really honored, too."

Murphy enjoyed his finest season in 1983 while the Redskins were on their way to a second straight Super Bowl, when he led the NFL by collecting nine of his 27 career interceptions, was named All-Pro, and was selected to play in the Pro Bowl. "I was kind of at the point where I think mentally, I was experienced enough where I really understood exactly what offenses were trying to do to us," said Murphy, who spent eight seasons in Washington. "Physically, I was still at a high level, and I think the other thing is obviously we had an outstanding team. We got big leads, and our defensive line was putting great pressure on the quarterback. So it all came together. I was just very fortunate the way things worked out."

Sidelined by Quinine

Chosen in the ninth round of the 1982 NFL Draft out of Southwest Texas State, Ken Coffey's journey to Washington's playing field would take a detour through the training room. "Basically, I found out I'm not compatible with quinine [which is used in medicine for the treatment of muscle cramps]," said the safety. "We played our first two [preseason] games that year in Miami and Tampa, and as you know, that's probably not the easiest places to play in August. A lot of players had cramps. I just lost a lot of playing time as a result of becoming dehydrated.

"And lo and behold, I had this allergic reaction to quinine, where it makes me nauseous. And that was the first thing that was manifested. The second thing was, as I became nauseous and was hurling, I was losing fluids. [The medical staff] thought they'd better stabilize me. So they gave me an IV and unfortunately, the first time they did it, they hit an artery as opposed to a vein. We got it stabilized and they put a band-aid on it, but it wouldn't stop bleeding. It turned out that quinine took my blood platelets out. It was pretty scary."

Ending up on the Redskins' injured-reserve list, the quinine-free Coffey practiced with the team and tried to pick up the game's nuances from veteran safeties Mark Murphy and Tony Peters. "It basically gave me an opportunity to learn the system and be kept around," said Coffey, who would go on to play four seasons in Washington. "All things happen for a good purpose, and this was clearly one of them."

Green's Start to Stardom

The prestige of being the first-round draft choice of the defending Super Bowl champion comes with varying questions.

The player, of course, is excited because he's being given the opportunity to join the proven best team in the NFL. But he has to take into account that the team just won the Lombardi Trophy with the players that they had. Why do they need him? And just how much will he get to play?

When the Redskins made Texas A&M cornerback Darrell Green their top pick in 1983, less than three months after winning Super Bowl XVII, nine-year veteran Jeris White was the starting left cornerback and had co-led the team in interceptions with the starting right cornerback, Vernon Dean.

Cornerback Darrell Green spent 20 seasons with the Redskins and was inducted into the Pro Football Hall of Fame in 2008.

What were Green's expectations when he arrived at Washington's training camp? "To try to get a starting job, make the team, try to start. I don't know if you call those expectations as much as hopes, dreams," Green said in *Warpath.* "My mindset, I think, was a little different from this generation, proven by the fact that the guy who was drafted right after me was cut. That was part of the normal world, because his [signing] bonus was probably $100,000. Mine was $300,000. You weren't thinking, 'I'm here, I'm doing great.' You were thinking, 'Man, I've got to try to hustle to make the team.' And then my goal was to try to get a starting job."

While Green did well on defense during camp, the speedster turned some heads on special teams when he returned a punt 61 yards for a touchdown the first time he touched the ball in the preseason opener against Atlanta.

It was, however, a contract dispute by White that put the rookie in the starting lineup against Dallas in the season opener on September 5. And just as was the case in the preseason game against the Falcons, Green was at the center of attention again when, during the nationally televised Monday night game, he chased down and tackled Cowboys star running back Tony Dorsett from behind. "My classmates and I talked about that in college just months before," said Green. "'What does Dorsett bring? Do you think you can catch him?' The world saw that, that was the first game, Monday night."

Starting every game as a rookie, Green collected a pair of interceptions during the regular season and had a team-high 79 solo tackles. He added a 72-yard interception return for a touchdown against the then–Los Angeles Rams in the playoffs and was named to the Associated Press and *Football Digest* all-rookie teams.

Rookie Season: Take Two!

Suffering a broken left wrist during his second preseason game and being placed on injured reserve by the Bills in 1988 offered cornerback Martin Mayhew an opportunity to begin his rookie season all over again. However, because of Plan B free agency, the fresh start would occur in Washington instead of Buffalo.

"Plan B free agency was pretty much to protect your top 37 players and free everybody else up. And so I was one of the guys who was freed up," said Mayhew. "I traveled around to several teams that were interested in signing me, so I felt pretty confident that I had a chance to play in this league.

"I looked at the Redskins as a team that definitely had a need at corner, more so than the other teams. And from talking with their coaches, Emmitt Thomas and Richie Petitbon, they really felt that I had a good chance to contribute early on and thought I could help out the team a lot. So that's why I decided to go with them.

"And they had just won a Super Bowl a couple of years before that and a lot of those players were still around. So I felt that they had a chance to be a championship-caliber team."

Contributing mostly on special teams during the first half of the 1989 campaign, Mayhew moved into the starting lineup in the 10th game of the year against Philadelphia and helped the Redskins notch six wins out of their last seven games.

"Darrell [Green] had an injury and was out for the season. And then we had another player who was suspended by the league and was out," Mayhew said. "So myself and another rookie, A.J. Johnson, ended up starting pretty much the whole second half of the season. It was great because when I finished playing [at Florida State], I didn't think I'd even have an opportunity to be drafted. So I was ecstatic about the opportunity I had to play."

If that was the case, Mayhew must have been euphoric when the 1990 season kicked off and he was starting at left cornerback. He would lead the Redskins with seven interceptions. "I wasn't a rookie anymore and I kind of understood the game a lot better," said Mayhew. "And I really had opportunities to make plays because nobody wanted to throw at [the other starting cornerback] Darrell Green. So I was getting every throw. I gave up some touchdowns, too. It wasn't a Pro Bowl year, but I made some plays when teams decided to pick on me. It wasn't really that new to me because I played with Deion [Sanders] at Florida State. I got kind of the same treatment there, so I was used to it.

"You just have to come to the game ready to play and just know that on the first third down, hey, you know exactly where [the ball's] going.

It's coming your way, so be ready for it! It makes you study more, it makes you figure out what types of routes to expect. It makes you study the receivers more because you know you're going to get a lot of opportunities to make plays."

Benefited from the Surroundings

Following two seasons in Minnesota where he started seven games and was a standout on special teams, Brad Edwards became a free agent in 1990. The safety was happy that the Redskins showed interest in signing him and flattered that head coach Joe Gibbs was the one holding out a pen. "My first impression of him was on the phone when he called me directly about coming there," said Edwards. "We had a great conversation, and he was a very good communicator, very matter-of-fact, but very positive. He really kind of sold me right off the bat.

"Even though the Vikings had been to four Super Bowls, they hadn't won any of them. And so they really didn't have that feather in their cap, if you will. That was what the Redskins had, and there's something that inures to the benefit of an organization when they won that game. There was not an aura of arrogance by any means. It was just a confidence about the organization that was appealing."

Playing in the nickel defense and leading Washington's special teams with 112 hits during his first season, Edwards moved into the starting lineup at free safety in 1991. He helped the Redskins garner a 14–2 record and win the NFC East for the first time since walking away with the Lombardi Trophy following the 1987 campaign.

"There was an excellent nucleus of veteran players who had been in the system for a long time," Edwards said. "There was a very high level of consistency that was attributable to that organization. With the nucleus of coaches, front office, and core players, I think that as much as anything led to the stability and ultimate chemistry that was built, which lent itself to the success that the team had."

Besides "ultimate chemistry," a larger trophy case had to be built, as well. The Redskins needed more space after winning the Super Bowl XXVI championship over the Buffalo Bills.

Edwards was just getting warmed up. In 1992 he had a team-leading and career-high six interceptions and 157 return yards. "Having been in a situation where you're playing in the same system for a couple of years, you're really starting to get things down: all the defenses, all the checks, all the adjustments. All those things are starting to become second nature to you. You're thinking less about the call and who's supposed to line up where and who's supposed to cover who. You're thinking more of, 'How can I put myself in the best position to make plays?' And we had an excellent defense. We had excellent players, and so you're a beneficiary of those elements."

Winding Down a Wonderful Career

Five days before the Redskins were set to open the 2001 season on September 9 in San Diego, cornerback Darrell Green, who was entering his 19th season, made an announcement. "A couple of years ago I signed a contract to play five more years. At that time, [team owner Daniel] Snyder said this is a lifetime contract. I say that to say I'm not being run out of the league," said Green. "I'm still a part of a vibrant effort to win the championship. The coach [Marty Schottenheimer] is expecting me to participate this year. I had a good, tough fight for the starting job, and I'm looking forward to winning a Super Bowl.

"However, there are times in all of our lives when we have the ability or the opportunity to effect change. And in those times, those who are in position to do so must act in that moment.

"Before I move on with what's really important to me, officially I will say that at the end of the 2001–2002 season with the Washington Redskins, you will have seen me play my last professional football game. Namely, I will be retiring at the end of this football campaign."

Green, well, changed his mind and returned for season number 20 in 2002. "I wasn't looking for 20 years. I wasn't looking for 20 years last year. I was retiring because I wasn't counting the years," Green said in *Warpath*. "I was thinking about reaching my goals and trying to accomplish the broader goals that I had in life, in terms of my own family, my foundation, the support, the level of visibility, the financial strength. It was all those things that were important to me. I wasn't saying, 'I need to get 20 years,' or, 'I need to get five years.' It was one year at a time."

Listed lower on the team's depth chart than any other time in his career, Green still suited up for every game, making four starts. And while not collecting an interception all season was a first for him, another first occurred on November 28 when the Redskins traveled to Dallas to meet the Cowboys on Thanksgiving. "For the first time in my career I did not touch the field on defense. It really hurt. [Defensive coordinator Marvin Lewis] had a tough job here, bringing all these new guys in, the expectations that were on him. I think the thing that probably hurt the most was that I wasn't aware of it. I wasn't aware that this was a possibility that I wouldn't play in the game. Even now, the nickel spot belongs to [Rashad] Bauman, but [Lewis] never really officially told me, even though I asked him a couple times. I said, 'Hey, are we making the switch? Just tell me.' It's not so much, 'Don't do it!' Just tell me. He never did. I struggled with that a lot."

Washington's all-time leader in games played (295) continued. "But the rest of it, I pretty much was prepared for," Green said. "There's nothing like that moment when you're not playing as much, particularly when you don't know you're not playing as much. I've always been kind of in control. I knew every step of the way, but because of the way he played it out, he didn't really tell me. I think I was really shocked in Dallas.

"[But] I leave with zero regrets. No regrets. No hard feelings, no nothing. It's all joy. It's been a joyous career, including this year. It has been a joyous experience across the board. All the tons of people I've met in this business, all the experiences I've had, the memories. In my opinion, it's second to none."

In his first year of eligibility, Green, Washington's all-time interception leader (54), was inducted into the Pro Football Hall of Fame in 2008.

chapter 13

Called "Special" for a Reason

"The King"

Not being chosen during the 1970 draft may have been the best thing that could have happened to Rusty Tillman. As a free agent, he had the opportunity to pursue a tryout with any team in the league. But when one of those teams is being led by a football legend who has shown interest in you, well, then it's a no-brainer where to chase your dream of playing in the NFL.

"As a free agent, I had several alternatives where I wanted to go, and it came down between the Giants and the Redskins," said Tillman, a 6′2″, 230-pound linebacker from Northern Arizona. "And I wanted to play for Vince Lombardi. He was my idol as a kid, and I wanted to play for him. It was as simple as that."

Unfortunately, Lombardi passed away on September 3, 1970, 17 days before the season opened. Distressed but determined, Tillman, who had beaten the odds by making the Redskins, experienced what professional football life in Washington had to offer on and off the field. "It was amazing for me, being from a little town in Arizona to being in the nation's capital. I used to go every Monday and visit the monuments and stuff like that. It was just a real thrill, being involved with the Redskins," he said.

The Redskins would be coached by another football legend beginning in 1971 when George Allen arrived in Washington after having been the head coach of the Rams for five seasons. His reputation preceded him and concerned Tillman. "We heard that he liked veteran football players, so all of us young guys were running a little scared," Tillman said. "But when it came down to the final cut, I made it, and it was great playing for George. He probably kept me in the league as long as I was in."

Tillman played for eight seasons in Washington, seven under Allen, and was nicknamed "the King" because of his performance on special teams. Having played seven different special-teams positions, he helped the Redskins earn the NFC championship in 1972 and was a team captain from 1974 through his final season in 1977.

"We just wanted to make a difference," said Tillman. "We realized early on how important [special teams] was to George. He emphasized the kicking game so much, we all just decided that we were going to make a difference. And we did!"

A Special Special-Teams Player

A pulled hamstring during his rookie season under coach Otto Graham in 1968, coupled with a separated shoulder the following year under coach Vince Lombardi, was certainly not how Bob Brunet had hoped to begin an NFL career. Those injuries kept the disheartened running back out of Washington's lineup for a majority of the games.

His future looked more encouraging, however, with George Allen's arrival in 1971. The new coach acknowledged the importance of special teams, and Brunet would soon earn appreciation for being a special special-teams player. "I recognized my lot in the NFL early and found out I was not durable enough to be a regular and run the ball 15 to 20 times. Unlike John Riggins, who was so durable, he could run the ball 35 to 40 times a game and not have a scratch. I'd run the ball 15 times and had to go to an emergency room with my nose flattened out and eyes hanging out on the side of my face," laughed Brunet. "Then George Allen came along and starts doing his thing on special teams, and I found my niche.

"The year we went to the Super Bowl, 1972, in the preseason, I led the whole NFL in rushing and then I backed Larry [Brown] at halfback and Charley [Harraway] at fullback [during the regular season]. So that tells you that George didn't believe in substituting a lot. His chronology of importance insofar as the three facets of the team: defense, of course, was No. 1; special teams were No. 2; and offense was No. 3.

"But I was one of his boys on the special teams, and to him it was almost a demotion to let me play offense. Even though I asked him on several occasions and said, 'Coach, I can do both.' He was the first guy in the NFL to have a full-time special-teams coach."

Future Hall of Fame coach Marv Levy held that job on Allen's staff in 1971 and 1972. "I really think a lot of Marv. He is a class guy," Brunet said. "We went from the Lombardi era and being last in the NFC in special teams to when George came and all of a sudden catapult to No. 1. We took a lot of pride in that."

Houston, You Caused Your Own Problem

In kicker-speak, Mark Moseley's route to the Redskins clanked off the crossbar about 100 times. Maybe 200 times. In other words, it wasn't a clean kick that sailed through the uprights.

After he spent the 1970 season with the Philadelphia Eagles, who had drafted him that year in the 14th round, Moseley moved back to his native Texas and played the following year in Houston. His Oilers career, however, came to an abrupt close a day after they were beaten by Denver in the 1972 season opener, 30–17.

"It's kind of a long story, but I got blackballed," said Moseley. "When they fired [Ed Hughes as the head coach following the 1971 season], they hired Bill Peterson, who was supposed to be this big, hotshot college coach from Florida. He cut me after the first game [Moseley was 1-for-2 on field-goal attempts and 2-for-2 on extra points]. He was using me as an example because we got beat by the Broncos and he thought he had to cut somebody. So he cut me! I came in on Monday morning, and he was in the parking lot and called me over and said, 'I waived you this morning.' So I went in and started packing my bags and none of the [assistant] coaches or even the general manager even knew that he waived me.

"I got a call from the Browns that very day, and they wanted me to come to Cleveland and do the place-kicking so that Don Cockroft could just punt. They said they'd be sending me a ticket and would get back with me in a couple hours. They never did. [Years later] I asked [Cleveland's general manager] what happened. He said, 'When we talked to the Oilers, they said you were washed up, that you were finished. We didn't even bother following up on it. It was our mistake, but that's what happened.' Several teams had actually talked to the Oilers, and they bad-mouthed me from the standpoint that they just didn't want me back in the league because they knew if I went somewhere else and shined, it would really make them look bad."

With a 1–13 record, the Oilers looked bad on their own. Moseley, meanwhile, looked for work. He spent the remainder of the 1972 campaign and all of the 1973 season contacting every team in the NFL. In 1974 he received a reply from Redskins head coach George Allen.

"He remembered that I kicked [two] field goals against the Redskins in a driving rainstorm at RFK Stadium [while with the Oilers on October 10, 1971]," Moseley said. "So he had his camera guy, who was Nate Fine at the time, go back and find out who that kicker was. [Allen] called me up and asked me if I had been training and wanted to play again. I said yeah, I was ready, and so he sent me a contract. I showed up in July in Carlisle [Pennsylvania] for training camp and competed against 12 other guys for the job and ended up getting it."

And how did the apparently rust-free Moseley earn the job and make his way back onto an NFL team's roster? "I think more than anything, I just never wavered," he said. "I always had a lot of confidence in my ability. And then when I came in there, I was kicking the ball very well. And as I improved, I just kind of knocked the kickers off one at a time and I went through the preseason without any misses. I made 16 in a row. That kind of impressed [Allen].

"But I almost lost it! I screwed up against the Giants [in the 1974 season opener]. We played at Yale Stadium, and the grass was really, really deep. They hadn't mowed it, and it was three or four inches deep. It was hard getting the ball out of the grass, and I missed two field goals just before halftime that were back-to-back. I missed one and had a penalty and got to try again and hit the crossbar. I thought they were going to cut me after that, but they didn't. I had a good special-teams coach that said, 'Let's give him a chance to work his way in here.' And sure enough, I did."

A Great Returner from the Great White North

When Redskins general manager Bobby Beathard was seeking a return specialist prior to the 1980 season, he didn't exactly look for help from the cavalry. But from the Rough Riders? Well, that's a different story.

After playing for three seasons in the Canadian Football League, the last two with the Ottawa Rough Riders, Mike Nelms' abilities on special teams came to Beathard's attention. "Bobby Beathard supposedly 'discovered' me in Canada," laughed Nelms. "He called and spoke with Willie Wood, who had coached at one time in Toronto, and he gave me a good referral. So based on that, Bobby gave me favorable numbers [in a contract], what I was asking for when I came."

During his first season in Washington, Nelms' contract was not the only place where the numbers were favorable. He returned 38 kickoffs for a 21.3-yard average and averaged 10.1 yards on 48 punts. Beathard's "discovery" was noticed around the league, and he was selected to play in the Pro Bowl. "I was just surprised! I never even thought about making All-Pro," Nelms said. "It never crossed my mind. I was just trying to do the best I could do. Someone handed me the wire that came across the teletype. It was a slip of paper that had all the players' names on it that had been voted All-Pro. It was out of the clear blue sky. It was cool. I never considered it, never thought about it. And then, there it was. I was pretty excited and elated about it. After that, I was going for it from then on."

He stuck to his word. The following season, in 1981, he led the NFL in kick returns with a 29.7 average. His punt average also improved, and he tied a Redskins record by returning two for touchdowns, including a career-high 75-yarder against the New England Patriots on October 25. "When I caught it, I knew there was somebody real close to me," Nelms said. "I had a sense that he was right there in front of me, and normally I like to make the catch and step to one side or the other. But he was so close, all I could do was catch it and duck my head. My helmet hit him right in the chest, and when he hit me, I stood up real hard and he came off.

"At that point, I just started going straight ahead, and the wall [of blockers] was right in front. I had some of our people to the left and some to the right, and all I had to do was go right between them. It was like running through a tunnel. I made it through and then I looked up and saw the punter. And then I saw that [Terry] Metcalf had an angle on him, so I just made a little move, and the guy was behind me."

Nelms, who was named to the Pro Bowl following the first three of his five seasons with the Redskins, feels there are at least a couple reasons why he was a successful kick and punt returner. "People sometimes say being crazy helped. But I considered my strengths to be quickness and being deceptively strong," said the 6'1", 188-pound Nelms. "I think I was stronger than most people thought I was. You don't have to be the strongest; you just need to be stronger than they think you are. And then use it to your advantage. It's like, never underestimate somebody's intelligence, and never underestimate some guy's speed. It's best to never underestimate your opponent. I think often that my strength was underestimated, as well as my balance and determination."

MVP: The M Stands for Moseley

The Redskins and veteran place-kicker Mark Moseley crested at the same time. In 1982 Washington went 8–1 during the strike-shortened season, beat its division-rival Dallas Cowboys to capture the NFC crown, and then dumped the Miami Dolphins to earn the Super Bowl XVII championship.

Moseley, in his ninth season with the Redskins, was nearly perfect. Successful on a league-leading 20-of-21 field-goal attempts, he added 16 PATs to total 76 points. And for the first and only time in the history of the NFL for a kicker, he was named as the league's Most Valuable Player. "I'm very proud of that year," said Moseley. "I'm proud of almost my entire career because I don't think I ever slacked. I was one of those guys that worked my hardest all the time to be the best that I can be and give everything that I had to my team to help them win. That's probably what I'm most proud of. But I think that year of '82 because of what it meant to our team, had I not been kicking as well as I was, we would not have ever even made the playoffs that year. But as it was, it got us to the playoffs, and then our offense kicked into gear after that, and we just breezed through the playoffs and got to the Super Bowl and won it."

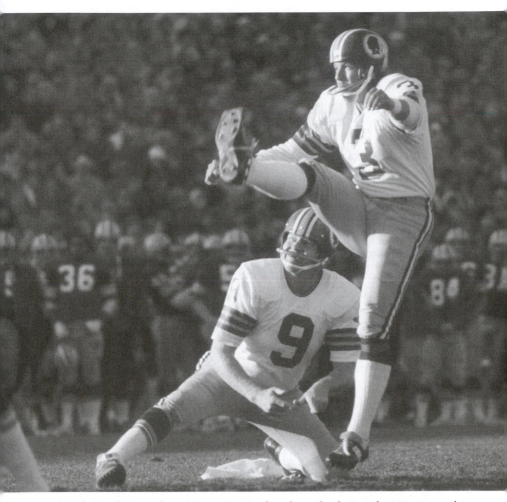

Mark Moseley won the NFL MVP Award in the strike-shortened 1982 season, the only place-kicker ever to do so. Photo courtesy of Getty Images

While the Redskins returned to but lost in the Super Bowl the following year, Moseley's performance during the regular season was brilliant. Converting on 33 of 47 field-goal attempts, and 62 of 63 PATS, Moseley set an NFL scoring record for a place-kicker with 161 points.

"Those years, from '79 to about '84, were really peak years for me," said the two-time Pro Bowler, who holds the team's career record with

1,206 points. "I was hitting the ball as well as anybody's ever hit the ball in the NFL. I was just at the peak and [during that period, no matter] where you'd give me the ball, wherever it was, I could make it. I hit two 50-yard field goals in one game [on October 26, 1980, against New Orleans], which was the first time a kicker had done that. So I was just peaking at a good time, when the team really needed me."

High Expectations

Washington was spoiled. For 13 seasons, 1974 to 1986, Mark Moseley handled the kicking duties. It was a done deal.

The Super Bowl XXII champion Redskins hoped to duplicate that stability in 1988 when they selected Chip Lohmiller with their top draft pick. And while high-round choices are generally under the microscope and pressured to produce quickly in order to show they are NFL- and big paycheck–worthy, that increases tenfold for a kicker. Like a quarterback, the kicker is the center of attention whenever he steps onto the field. His performance has an immediate pass-fail evaluation.

"I was very excited to come there to a Super Bowl team with a winning tradition and play under Coach [Joe] Gibbs. But I definitely had pressure on me to perform well," said Lohmiller, who was chosen in the second round, 55th overall. "The expectations of the team were very high.

"After I made the team, I had to do my duty and contribute and try not to miss any field goals. I just had to go out there and do my job and try to be calm about it. Being a rookie and being under the limelight in Washington is pretty tough. You just have to go with what you've done in the past and do your best."

Lohmiller followed his own advice. During his rookie season, he kicked three game-winning field goals, including one in division rival Philadelphia's Veterans Stadium on December 4. The Redskins went home with a 20–19 victory.

"I kicked a 44-yard field goal against the wind [with only one second left in the game] to win it when [Eagles head coach] Buddy Ryan was running off the field. He didn't think I was going to make it."

The More You Can Do...

As Washington's 1990 preseason opened against Atlanta on the University of North Carolina campus in Chapel Hill on August 11, head coach Joe Gibbs barely had enough time to adjust the headset over his hat when he spotted a rookie who would become his return specialist.

Brian Mitchell, a quarterback from Southwestern Louisiana who was drafted in the fifth round, was being converted to running back and more specifically into a kickoff and punt returner. He caught the opening kickoff from the Falcons and returned the ball 92 yards for a touchdown.

The rookie's celebration, however, was fleeting. The time that it took Mitchell to race the ball nearly the entire length of the field was roughly how long he had to feel confident that that return effort secured him a spot on the Redskins' roster. "Well, I was thinking that it did," Mitchell laughed. "All the players when I came to the sideline were saying that, and [special-teams coach] Wayne Sevier basically told me I hadn't done a damn thing yet. Get on the football field, I was on the kickoff team, and I'd better be able to tackle."

Throughout training camp, Mitchell, like most every rookie, had to try to impress his coaches. But he had to do so with the added burden of playing at an unfamiliar position. "I was a little nervous because I had played quarterback for nine years [in high school and college] and I always had the mindset that return guys were crazy. It's a tough job I never thought would be my job. But I always tell people having that success that early probably made me want to do it and begin to work more at it. Because if I didn't have that success, I probably would have left and went to Canada and try to play quarterback."

As the regular season was set to open, Mitchell could shelve any thoughts about clearing customs at the border because he had earned a place on the team and was a Redskin.

Contributing almost entirely on special teams through the first eight games, while Washington practiced for its November 12 meeting with the Eagles in Philadelphia, Mitchell took a step back into his past and went under center as a quarterback. "Going into that game, [the starting quarterback Mark] Rypien was already hurt, and we had Stan

Humphries and Jeff Rutledge [as backups]. Both of those guys got hurt in the game," said Mitchell. "And that week they had just happened to give me a shortened version of the game plan and told me to be prepared if something was to happen to them. And it just so happened [in] that game that the four people that I backed up, those two at quarterback, and Walter Stanley and Joe Howard Johnson at punt return, all four of them got hurt!"

And so, while Murphy's Law dictated Mitchell's offensive debut in the NFL, it occurred during a nationally televised *Monday Night Football* broadcast, no less. "When I walked into the huddle, I basically told them that on this first play I'm going to do what I always did in college, I'm going to roll out and act like I'm going to pass and I'm going to run the football," said Mitchell, who as an option quarterback in college, passed for 1,966 yards and rushed for 1,311 yards during his senior season. "They were very supportive. It was a game where we were having a tough time. I think nine total people got hurt that day. So we were just thinking, I guess, let's try and get though this game and see what we can do. I think the next person in line [to play quarterback] was Russ Grimm."

While Grimm stayed put at right guard, Mitchell finished the 28–14 loss as Washington's quarterback. In his only series, he completed three passes for 40 yards, had two rushes for 11 yards, and scored on a run from the 1-yard line. He also led the Redskins with 12 hits on special teams.

Mitchell's Super in the Dome

Brian Mitchell provided an excellent reason why home cooking should not be underestimated when the Redskins traveled to his native Louisiana on September 11, 1994, to play against the New Orleans Saints in the Superdome. "I told guys, 'You know, I've had a lot of success in that stadium.' When I was in college [at Southwestern Louisiana], I had a lot of success there," Mitchell said. "And going into the game and having the blocking that we had, our special teams, we took pride in trying to go out there and give our team a boost. It just happened for us there. I guess some stadiums are just good for people. Whenever I played in New Orleans or I played in Philadelphia, I just had a knack or had a feeling that something good was going to happen, and it did that day."

Did it ever! First he returned a punt 74 yards for a touchdown. And later in the game, he had an 86-yard kickoff return that set up another touchdown that helped Washington beat New Orleans, 38–24.

On those two and on all of his returns, there was a plan. "I tried to get right back [down the field] as fast as I could. I didn't want to have many wasted movements," said Mitchell, who gained 225 all-purpose yards against the Saints and was named the NFC Special-Teams Player of the Week. "I didn't want to go side to side, I was trying to catch the ball and immediately get back into it, which gave me the advantage. If I come back into the coverage team, and they start breaking down, I know that my blockers have a chance of blocking them.

"If it was called a right return, a left return, or a middle return, I stuck to that return because that in turn would limit the amount of penalties you're going to get. And also, your guys will know where you're always going to be, you knew where they were going to be [and because of that] you had a more successful return game."

Mitchell enjoyed a successful career as a returner for the Redskins. The team's all-time leader with 317 punt returns for 3,476 yards, he returned seven for touchdowns. He also holds Washington's all-time kick-return records with 421 returns for 9,586 yards.

chapter 14

Inside the Beltway

"[Redskins owner] Edward Bennett Williams had a chauffeur named Leroy. [My attorney and I arrived in D.C. following the draft], and he said, 'Leroy, show them around.' Leroy says, 'Do you want to see the Supreme Court?' So Leroy just double-parks in the middle of the street, and all the security guards, park police, and whoever come up and say, 'Oh, Leroy. How are you doing?'

"So we go into the Supreme Court Building, and the justices are hearing a case, so we stand in the back. Leroy says, 'Hey, you want to see the chambers?' I said, 'Sure,' because [Judge Byron] 'Whizzer' White was an All-American at [my alma mater] the University of Colorado. He says, 'Okay, let's go to Judge White's office.' So we go through the room where they put on their black robes and into Judge White's personal, private chambers, and Leroy's just showing us around. 'Here's his closet. Here's his desk where he makes all his decisions.' It was pretty awesome.

"We get back, and I meet with [coach Vince] Lombardi. They have a press conference, and this guy comes up and puts a chair in front of me and stands up on the chair. He said, 'I need to interview you.' He was so short that when he stood up on the chair he was still about my height. So we go through the interview, he steps off the chair and turns to the camera and says, 'This is Warner Wolf, talking with the biggest Redskin of all.' That was the first time I met Warner Wolf."

—Bill Brundige, defensive lineman

•

"Well, I do have a lot of fond memories of being there and some of the things that took place. I went to the White House a lot with different presidents. I was at a state dinner one night and sat with Ronald Reagan and chatted with him about a lot of different things. One of the things I was talking with him about [while] sitting at the table, I told him that he looked good. He said, 'You know, I've lifted weights since I've been in the White House. They have a nice weight room with machines that I can work out on.' And he said, 'I've put three or four inches on my chest.' I said, 'God, you look great!' And he said Nancy's father was a doctor and prescribed this multivitamin for him. He said, 'It's very good, Sonny. You should take this.' And I said, 'I certainly will. I see what it's doing for you.' And he gave me the name of it. And the next day and a half, I guess, in the mail, I get a note from him telling me that, 'I remember what I told you about the multivitamin and the name of the multivitamin I was taking. But it's been discontinued and I didn't want you out trying to look for it and saying, "What was he talking about?"'

"But I've gone to private dinners on Sunday nights when you look at movies and stuff with a few people, and it was nice. That's one of the nice things about being in the nation's capital playing. And, of course, the Redskins fans were great. They were great to me and they've been great to all the Redskin players because they're passionate about the game, they love their team, and it was fun."

—Sonny Jurgensen, quarterback

•

"John F. Kennedy was president, and I remember playing touch football with him [and Bobby Kennedy on the White House lawn]. They did that all the time. Somebody in their office would call and say, 'Would you come over and throw a few?' And I did it. They were very, very athletic. They seemed so absorbed in whatever they were doing. It was just very impressive to me that they just worked as hard at that as they seemed to be working at everything else. The excitement of a young president, a young wife [Jacqueline], I remember Washington in those exciting times. A young player building a new team in a dynamic city, you couldn't ask for a better scenario.

"We were on the practice field when he was assassinated in Dallas [on November 22, 1963]. We were getting ready to play the Eagles and [coach Bill] McPeak called us together and said, 'We just got word that the president of the United States has just been assassinated.' It was just a shocking time.

"His wife and Bobby Kennedy said that he wouldn't want [the NFL to cancel that weekend's games]. So they just took a moment of silence before all the games in his memory. It was a tough time."

—Norm Snead, quarterback

.

"Washington was an exciting town to play in. Next to New York, it was probably the most exciting team to play for in the NFL. When you get the president at practice and you get senators and representatives and cabinet members and big-shot people at practice, that's powerful stuff.

"Dick Nixon. Gerald Ford. Nixon used to come to practice a couple of times a year. And we used to go to the White House quite often. We pretty well had a pass. I'd have people come in from out of town and I'd call ahead to the White House, and we could slip right in for a tour.

"I was going through there one night, and all of a sudden, a door opened up and a guy walked out in a military outfit and said, 'The president would like to see you.' It was Jimmy Carter then, and we had a little visit. He welcomed me to the White House, and we talked about the team a little bit, and he was on his way."

—Diron Talbert, defensive tackle

sources

Whittingham, Richard. *Hail Redskins: A Celebration of the Greatest Players, Teams, and Coaches*. Chicago: Triumph Books, 2004.

Carroll, Bob, Michael Gershman, David Neft, and John Thorn. Elias Sports Bureau. *Total Football: The Official Encyclopedia of the National Football League*. New York: HarperCollins Publishers, 1999.

Washington Post, *Washington Times*, Associated Press, *Warpath*, www.nfl.com, www.redskins.com, www.profootballhof.com.